COOKING OUT-OF-DOORS

COOKING OUT-OF-DOORS

GIRL SCOUTS OF THE U.S.A. / 830 THIRD AVE. / NEW YORK, N. Y. 10022

Catalog No. 19-984

This book was compiled by

ALICE SANDERSON RIVOIRE

Program Specialist, Program Department

designed by

GLORIA GENTILE

and the spot illustrations were drawn by

DENNY HAMPSON

CONTENTS

Over the years Girl Scouts

have developed skills in the art of outdoor cookery

that are of interest to Girl Scouts and non-Girl Scouts alike.

This book is therefore addressed to all those

who enjoy a picnic, a beach party, or a cookout

and want to broaden their cooking skills.

Each recipe serves 12, unless otherwise indicated.

1.
TO EVERYONE WHO ENJOYS EATING OUTDOORS

When someone says, "Let's eat out," you know that you are in for a treat without the routine kitchen chores. When you eat outdoors, there's an added tang to the food plus the satisfaction of being able to feed yourself, your friends, and your family without the familiar gadgets and equipment that we take for granted in our home kitchens.

1

IF YOU CAN COOK AT HOME, YOU CAN COOK OUTDOORS

If you can follow a recipe in a kitchen, you can certainly do it in the woods, at the beach, on the trail, or wherever you find yourself. Food is food, ingredients are ingredients, and measurements don't change just because they have blue sky instead of a roof over them. To cook you need heat. The experienced chef of a gas range has to learn the special techniques of an electric range and vice versa. In the same way, a cook in the out-of-doors must learn the secrets of an ember fire and how long it takes to boil water over it.

Because you frequently have to carry your own equipment and supplies for outdoor cooking, you soon learn which of the indoor items are superfluous and which have simple outdoor substitutes. Sometimes, this very simplicity of equipment and the challenge to ingenuity appeal to would-be cooks who have never been active in the kitchen at home. This book is designed to familiarize the novice cook with the ways of the outdoors. Of course, it is harder to teach a beginner to cook outdoors than in a modern kitchen, but it can be done. It means learning how to measure ingredients like flour on a windy day! Or taking time to reread a complicated recipe while the sand sifts into the stew pot!

BEGIN WITH SIMPLE MENUS

They say a word to the wise is sufficient. Just as a wader doesn't jump into 12 feet of water and expect to be able to swim, so the beginner in the out-of-doors doesn't start with a meal for which every item must be cooked over the coals. Planning is the secret to success. At first, prepare to take food that is ready to eat when you stop walking or riding. Next time add a simple food that needs only quick cooking—

like canned or dried soups, cocoa, tea or coffee for adults, and heated tomato juice or vegetable juice. These can be started as soon as the fire is lit, for the first flames are fine for heat, and the coals that come later finish the job.

In this book you will find many recipes for fireless foods and one-pot or skillet dishes. Even the superior outdoor chef makes use of these menu items in planning a meal. That superior brand of cook also has tried recipes in all the other categories in this book and really tested her skill by using the gimmicks and gadgets. Within each chapter you will find both the simple and the complicated. Be sure to read carefully when choosing a recipe to prepare.

PATIENCE IS THE KEY

Patience is the key to this choice. Remember that patience comes with experience and age. From *experience* you know what to expect; for example, how much firewood is really needed

and how long it takes to burn to a fine bed of coals. Or how long bread twists take to cook to crispness beyond the doughy, gummy stage. *Age* brings the ability to have patience based on that knowledge.

Few seven-year-olds are happy sitting still long enough to toast bread twists. This means holding that toasting stick steady and still over coals that took so long to change from flames to red lumps. Besides, the typical seven-year-old likes to *see* flames and *that* is what *she* calls a *fire*. She hasn't had enough experience to see the beauty in the shifting colors of the coals or to remember the taste treat of a well browned— not burned – marshmallow held quietly over those coals for at least 15 minutes while the older girls compared notes of the latest school news.

The younger you are the less interested you are in gathering enough wood for a long cooking process, in waiting for coals to come from

3

flames, in holding a long, awkward stick still and out of another cook's way. Physically, young arms, hands, and memories are not ready for these jobs. Young cooks like to see the flames of their fire, to watch their food cook and to eat almost immediately. The one-pot fits their needs along with giving them the chance to gain experience, which with age will increase their patience.

The older you are the more physically able you are to handle: the large wood supply; the wait for coals; the toasting fork and other implements; the wait for food to cook, even when out of sight—like dumplings under the kettle lid or the ham in the imu. When you know how much patience you have, you know what methods of cooking and types of recipes you can do successfully.

LEARN THE BASICS AND IMPROVISE

This book is designed to help you start as a beginner—no matter what your age—and to become an experienced outdoor cook as fast as your abilities, experience, and age will let you. These recipes are designed for 12 persons, since this is an easy number to increase to 24-36-48, etc. It is impossible to include all the favorite recipes and ideas of the outdoor cooks in this country. You can start with these, collect more from your friends, and create your own recipes to share with others. This book is the beginning of a trail to show you how; then you can blaze your own—right to the point where people say, "My, she's a good cook, indoors or out."

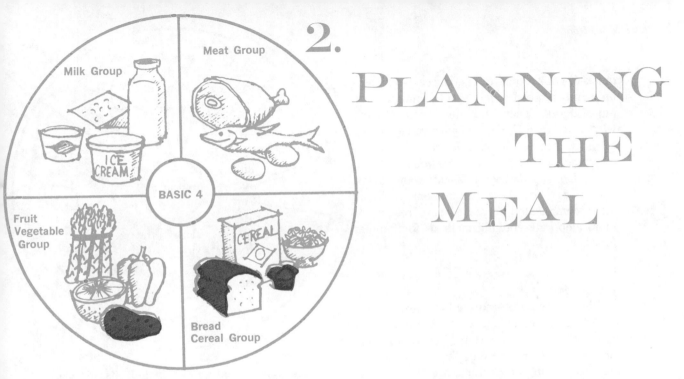

Milk Group

Meat Group

BASIC 4

Fruit
Vegetable
Group

Bread
Cereal Group

ICE CREAM

CEREAL

2. PLANNING THE MEAL

The meal you choose when you eat out will depend on why you want to eat it. Is it to keep up your strength for the many exciting things you are doing on the hike or in camp? The quick-to-cook, quick-to-eat, and easy-to-clean-up menu is in order. Are you learning to cook out-of-doors? Then you must keep in mind what you already know and what you are ready for next. Are you looking forward to proving to yourself and your friends that you are a good cook? Do you and your friends want to test yourselves? For these two reasons you pick more complicated forms of easy recipes or more elaborate cooking methods for familiar foods.

IMPORTANCE OF GOOD NUTRITION

Whatever may be required for a meal with regard to ingredients and preparation, good nutrition is always important. For groups planning either a single meal or three meals a day, the Basic Four food groups are easy guides. A more detailed guide is the Basic Seven food groups.

A single meal should include its share of these daily foods. Three meals a day can be built around the groups so that none are forgotten. Each meal should also have variety in taste (how would you like tomato juice, Blushing Bunny, tomato salad, and tomato soup cake?), and contrast and consistency in color (think of potato soup, creamed codfish on potatoes, cottage cheese salad, and vanilla pudding!).

PLACE AND CIRCUMSTANCE

Sometimes the surroundings and unexpected events dictate the type of meal. Fireless meals are in order during a fire ban in the woods, above the timberline in the mountains on a short trip, on a bus en route to camp, or as the midday repast on a rocky island during a canoe trip. One-pot dishes are called for where only soft wood is available. Soft woods will provide heat with a good flame but will never make coals. One-pot meals are also practical on the stove used on a camping trip across the country. On the other hand, when the earth is easy

to dig for a pit, you can try your skill with an imu.

If planning goes awry, there are limitless opportunities for improvisation. For example, if a stew is planned and someone has forgotten the kettle, cook in the aluminum foil the raw vegetables were packed in. Or if an oven is too awkward for your trip, have bread twists which can be cooked with hot coals and a thick toasting stick. If someone drops the egg carton, well just change the menu from fried to scrambled eggs. When the coal stove in the cabin is kept going day and night for heat, take advantage of an excellent opportunity for making old-fashioned baked beans. And when there is no refrigeration to keep fresh milk sweet, use dried or evaporated milk for cocoa or chocolate milk. Have roasted corn where water is too scarce and precious to boil corn in, and a walking salad and kabobs when there is no hot water for dishwashing.

7

3.
SPECIAL
ACTIVITIES
AND
CLIMES

Outdoor cooking is done in snow and sand; winter and summer; from the Atlantic to the Pacific; from the Canadian to the Mexican border; from the fresh water Great Lakes to the salty Caribbean; from sea level or below to a mile and higher above the sea; by campers afoot, on skis, with horses, aboard canoes, rowboats or schooners, and in station wagons; in woods, plains, or deserts. In making your overall plans you should certainly take into consideration the variety of activity and, of course, location. (There are specialized books by persons who concentrate on just one area or type of camping.) In planning menus for specialized situations the Basic Four (or Seven) still applies.

AT HIGH ALTITUDES

High altitudes affect the form of foods in each of the basic groups, if boiling or baking is the method chosen. For cakes and hot breads it is wise to buy only mixes that are designed for the altitude or which give special directions for use. Since flour dries out more at the high altitudes, most baking recipes must have added liquid. And because the air pressure is less on the surface of the baking product, breads or cakes rise faster than at lower altitudes—so the leavening agent must be reduced along with some of the other tenderizing materials such as shortening and sugar.

Less air pressure also means that water can boil more easily—that it does not have to get to 212°F. before it boils (bubbles breaking on the surface). Fortunately for sanitary dishwashing, even at 8,000-foot altitudes the temperature of "boiling" water is 196°F. Therefore boiling water is still a good indication that the rinse water is at least the necessary 170°F. for sanitary rinsing of dishes. This same temperature decrease accounts for the added time that may be needed to cook vegetables by boiling. At the lower boiling temperature you must allow more time, even for the traditional camp fare of boiled dried beans.

9

AT THE BEACH

Beaches with little protection from sun, sand, and wind, and perhaps a dearth of water call for covered containers for cooking. Cold beverages brought from home in insulated containers make the purest drinks. A spot protected from wind or a windless day might, with luck, assure a marshmallow or kabob without sand. Aluminum foil is a boon here, as is traditional pit cooking—perhaps in the form of a clam bake with steamed corn.

BACKPACK TRIPS

Backpack trips require such lightweight foods as these: dehydrated soups (provided there is a good water supply on the site); dried fruits (apricots, raisins, prunes, apples, dates, etc.), which are necessary for bulk and for the vitamins and minerals they contain; dried milk;

cheese; dried beef; specially pre-prepared mixes for such favorites as spaghetti and chili dishes. (See Appendix for more suggestions.)

CANOE TRIPS

Canoes have little extra space for additional supplies and equipment. Proper packing is important to prevent dampening of foods by spray, shipped water, and rain and to avert premature broiling of food unprotected from the sun. Careful balancing of the load is also necessary to please the paddlers as well as for the sake of safety.

AUTO CAMPING

Groups or families traveling by auto are limited more by space than by weight; it is, therefore, often practical to carry one of the small ice chests or insulated boxes for food. The type of camp site or picnic area should determine what menus to plan. An emergency supply might well include dried or evaporated milk, canned soups and/or specialities like pork and beans, tea and instant or regular coffee for adults, depending upon the equipment. The simplest family meal out-of-doors is probably carried in a picnic basket and may be little different from the meals set out on the table at home for lunch or supper, with sandwiches, mixed salad, potato chips, milk or lemonade, and all the relishes.

For a stay of a week or two at a site or on a long auto journey, a kitchen box for storage and work surfaces is valuable. Opened up on lashed

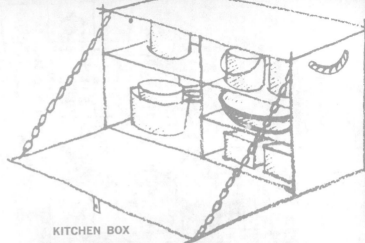

KITCHEN BOX

legs, set on the tailgate of a station wagon, or braced between trees, it becomes the kitchen cabinet in the outdoors and makes variety in the menu easier to achieve.

PACK TRIPS

Pack trips also require careful balancing of the load. Meals are influenced by the location of the trail and the camp site.

11

4.
"CONVENIENCE" FOODS

Emergency foods that require little or no cooking and come conveniently packed are ideal for outdoor cooking. Each year more and more "convenience" foods appear. Be sure to look carefully at them on your grocer's shelf next time. You will find mixes for baked goods and beverages, no-cook desserts, dried vegetables and condiments. Outdoor cooks rarely use frozen foods unless there is a freezer to keep the foods frozen or unless the food can be used before thawing.

Try these "convenience" foods at home first — taste test. Then, for each package that is more expensive than the raw ingredients would be, decide whether the time, equipment, effort, or weight saved overbalances the extra cost.

A good cook knows how to cook from a book and also from the box; she can decide for herself which one she wishes to use, depending upon time, money, ingredients, equipment, and energy she has on hand. There are even homemade mixes for the cook who wants to "make her own" but likes the convenience of a mix for such things as biscuits and cocoa at mealtime. A cook who can prepare a meal from only a box and the one who scorns boxes in favor of books are both halfway cooks. Each still has a lot to learn about the other's way in order to make smart choices of what to use for a particular meal.

CIVIL EMERGENCIES

These "convenience" foods are suggested by Civil Defense groups in their instructions for emergency menus when natural disasters of wind, weather, and water, or man-made catastrophes have disrupted gas and electricity in homes. Many local and state units of Civil Defense provide three-day emergency menus for families based on these foods as well as directions on the mass feeding type of outdoor cooking with improvised equipment. Because of their confidence and practice, experienced outdoor cooks are especially valuable in such efforts. For a family emergency shelf, choose foods that can be eaten cold if necessary, quench thirst, satisfy hunger, and supply essential food values (Basic Four or Seven).

13

5.
FIRES

TEPEE FIRE

NO. 10 TIN-CAN STOVE

The menu usually determines the type of fire, but sometimes circumstances permit of only one type of fire. This book contains a series of chapters, each devoted to a specific method of cooking and to the type of fire generally used for that method. No fire can burn without these three vital factors—oxygen, fuel, and a source of heat.

In softwood localities where hardwoods such as oak are unavailable, charcoal takes its place. For the use of charcoal in toasting and baking, be sure to read the relevant section in the chapter on ember cooking. Sometimes the source of heat is even more manmade—fuel in the family portable stove; wood or coal in a range.

In a cabin, most wood or coal burners can be kept going continually when you understand the operation of the dampers in the stove pipe or chimney and the draft which admits air (oxygen) for the fire.

FIRE SAFETY

Fire safety and conservation of natural resources go hand in hand. The small cooking fire no larger than the size of the pot or just large enough for the toasting forks to be used is the trademark of the good camper.

Check List for Fires

1. Choose fire to fit needs.
2. Choose a safe site.
   a. Secure permission to use site from owner.
   b. Clear enough space around the fire for safety.
   c. Avoid using shale rocks near fire. (Water between layers of these rocks tends to expand as it heats until the steam bursts the rock apart.)
   d. See that enough water and sand or extinguishing equipment is always on hand.
   e. Plan enough time for the fire to burn down.
   f. Take all precautions to be sure fire is

15

out. (A good test is to see if you can rest your hand on the ashes.)

    g. Plan enough time to erase the scar. (The larger the fire, the larger the scar.)

3. In order to avoid a burned patch on the grass and to cover the fire site effectively after cooking, cut a square of sod, lift off from the fire space, and place to one side on a canvas. Then water it occasionally. After the fire is completely extinguished and the area is cool, replace the squares of sod.

4. Gather wood — hardwood (elm, maple, oak) to make coals; softwood (pine, ash) for quick hot flames.

5. Start fire.

    a. Use waterproof matches; dip combustible end in melted wax or paint with nail polish. Store in metal box or can.

    b. Natural tinder for wood fires includes stalks of dried weeds, pine needles, fine dead twigs, shavings cut from dead sticks, bark from downed birches, huckleberry switches, and the like. For charcoal fires in wet weather and in terrain short of tinder, fire starters are a boon worth many times the small effort involved in making and carrying them. Tinder can also be made from wax and strips of cotton cloth 1 in. x 12 in. Just put strips into a can of wax shoe polish until wax is used up (any paste wax can be used); replace cover; remove strips as needed; place among kindling and ignite.

Excelsior, sawdust, or shavings with wax or paraffin are likewise good tinder substitutes. To prepare them for use, dry materials in an 8 in. x 8 in. pan; melt old candles or paraffin and pour over dry material until pan is full. When cool, saw into small squares and store in metal box. At site, insert in kindling and ignite.

c. **Puffer.** A stubborn fire can be given a boost with a puffer. A puffer can easily be made by attaching a metal tube about 3 in. long to one end of a rubber tubing (about 36 in. long). Insert the metal end under fire and puff from other end.

6. Campcraft books with detailed chapters on fires contain many additional suggestions.

6.
EQUIPMENT
AND
SAFETY

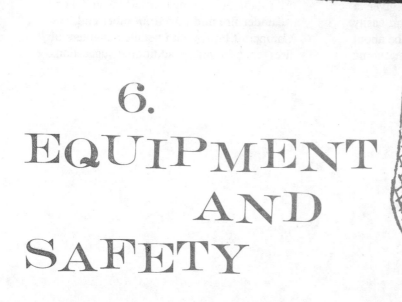

ORIOLE CACHE

Once the menu is chosen to fit your needs for a particular occasion and location, it is time to do your marketing and get your equipment in order.

EQUIPMENT LISTS

A choice of both menu items and their method of preparation will be governed by the equipment on hand. You make equipment lists based on what you want to eat and where you want to do it. *Start* with the utensils essential to any meal cooked outdoors—matches, jackknives (multi-purposed ones with can opener, etc.), first-aid kit, pot holders or gloves, the ever useful bandanna (apron, sit-upon, table mat, hand towel, costume, or puppet for after dinner programs).

Then list utensils by use—preparation (peeling, cutting, stirring, beating, mashing, turning, measuring); broiling; baking; serving (spooning, ladling, forking); eating (flat plate, cup, deep dishes); clean-up (scraping, rinsing, scalding silver, sanitizing dishes, sudsing, and air drying); storing and garbage disposal; fire extinguishing and transportation (by foot, horse, bicycle, auto, boat, canoes, etc.). When checking your list, see that you've included such important items as the "silver dunker" and mesh bag for sanitizing dishes.

Sometimes a utensil can do double or even quadruple duties—jackknives can pare, cut, open cans, lift bottle tops; large spoons stir, serve, and ladle; a cup measures, ladles, and can be used as a soup plate; deep dishes hold cereal with milk as well as supper hamburgers and peas. Utensils determine cooking time: deep narrow kettles take longer to boil; wide shallow pots that completely cover a fire cook quickly; two pots of water heat faster than the same quantity in one large pot. Utensils with bails are useful and can be adjusted on a crane to make the most of the fire's heat.

Between meals food still needs attention. Storage caches keep food dry, cold, fresh, antless, and away from bears or dogs. Cool things can be carried in containers wrapped in wet cloth or paper which cools by the evaporation process. Hanging caches should be dry or damp depending upon the food.

Typical equipment lists can be found in the Appendix. Use them to plan your meals, to estimate and arrange your packloads, to choose the forms of ingredients, to make substitutes for missing ingredients, etc.

SAFETY HINTS

PERSONAL SAFETY. There is no reason for deliberately making yourself uncomfortable outdoors. Proper clothes that afford protection from the weather (sun, rain, wind, heat, and cold, etc.) should be worn. Precaution against accidents can be taken by observing fire regulations (see Fire Check List), and using water that tests safe (is boiled 10 minutes or treated with purifier such as clorox or halazone tablets according to directions on the container).

PACK BASKET

When you must purify the water, it is usually more palatable as a beverage if you add chocolate milk mix, lemon juice, or powders or use it with cocoa or sassafras tea. If none of these flavorings are practical, try aerating it by shaking it when cool in its container or pouring it back and forth between two clean containers.

Pot holders or insulated picnic gloves—even cotton working gloves—prevent many an accidental burn. Tongs, long handled stirring spoons or forks keep hands at a comfortable distance from the heat. Can openers that are tested at home for efficiency, convenience, and workability are the only kind to take outdoors.

Knives that are kept sharp are safer than dull knives. In any case, always carry a first-aid kit.

SAFETY IN FOODS. Food entails safety factors too. Pick foods that will not spoil. Keep cold things cold and hot things hot—under 40° F. or over 140° F. Otherwise, choose foods that need no special care because of method of packing or protection (sterilized, dried, canned in air-tight containers, etc.). Leave at home or in the refrigerator such things as cooked custard, egg salad with mayonnaise, and potato egg salad, unless it will be no warmer than 40° F. until serving time. Fresh milk will not stay sweet long even at that temperature.

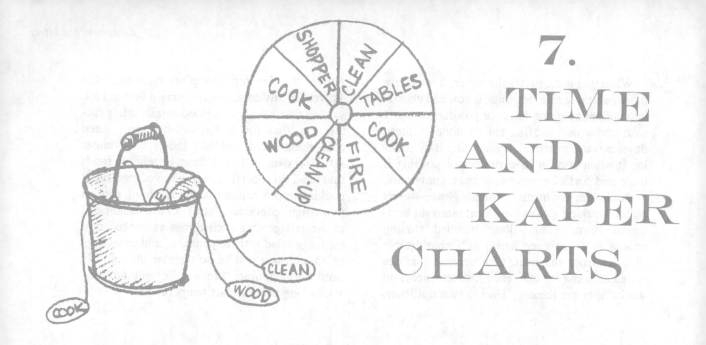

7.
TIME
AND
KAPER
CHARTS

When cooking is done for a family or other type of group, time and kaper charts are useful in organizing the work. Good planning gives a group time for other activities.

TIME CHARTS

A time chart is a handy way to plan the sequence of the various jobs that must be done. In setting up a time chart, consider the following:

To figure the time for a meal, remember to allow for the wood gathering, fire laying, lighting, and burning down to coals. Check the recipes for cooking time (and remember this assumes that your fire is constant and not alternately dying and flaring up because fuel isn't added properly). If preparation of the ingredients takes no longer than the fire preparation, you can overlap these duties; if it is a longer time, be sure to add that time to the total preparation time. Start with the menu item that takes the longest total time and then go on to the next longest, remembering that some things can be done by different persons at the same time. The time chart should also tell you how many persons are needed as cooks and when they need to start working.

KAPER CHARTS

A kaper chart is a technique for distributing the many necessary chores among the members of the group. In this way everyone shares the work. In addition to helping divide the chores fairly, kaper charts add to the fun of the occasion. Typical divisions of work can be based on the following plan: packers (marketeers); wood gatherers; fire builders; cooks; table arrangers; clean-ups. Kaper charts should be detailed and clear for the beginner and general for the experienced cook. The novice needs to know that dishwashing is part of clean-up and that it includes scraping, rinsing if feasible, washing in hot sudsy water, rinsing, and sanitizing in 170° F. or actively boiling water.

The cooks will be beloved by the clean-ups if, before putting the pots over the fire, they

23

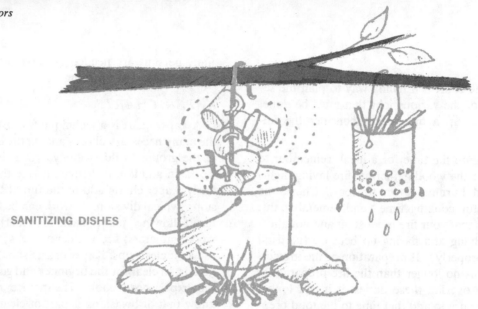

SANITIZING DISHES

soap the outsides of them with a bar of soap, coat them by hand with a paste of detergent and water, or paint them with a brush dipped in soap jelly made of leftover soap bits or other detergents. Cooks can be of further help if they put pots to soak with water when the serving is done and put kettles with dishwater over the fire.

24

8. FIRELESS FOODS

The recipes in this group do not require a fire, but they do have sparks of imagination, flavor, and fun. You may find yourself needing a fireless meal many times: for a quick meal on a hike; where fire bans prevent cooking; with a group of friends who have not yet learned to build a fire; during the heat of the day when no added heat is wanted; on a bus trip or a train; for the first meal at a camp site before there's time to build a fire.

In planning a cookout or camp meal smart beginners cook only one menu item and accompany it with fireless dishes—salads, desserts, sandwiches, etc. Sometimes, you want a snack in a fireless place. The no-cook puddings and other convenience foods and mixes are good under these circumstances, particularly if you can carry all the ingredients. Canned fruits are also a welcome treat. Some of these recipes travel well and are good in the nosebag.

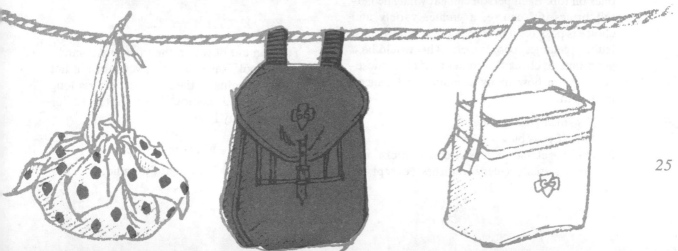

NOSEBAGS

When a horse is to be away from his quarters or grazing area, a thoughtful owner provides a bag of feed to hang conveniently on his bridle. You can carry your own personal "nosebag" made of a red bandanna, denim, plastic or paper bag. This holds the sandwiches, thirst quenchers, and dessert. Remember to pack heavy things at the bottom and light, crushable ones on top. Each person can eat what she herself brings. Of course, a greater variety and choice is possible if everyone pools sandwiches, fruit, vegetables, cookies, etc. This would be a good time to check the contents of each "nosebag" to see how many contained a balanced meal with:

1. Egg, meat, fish, or cheese.
2. Milk if possible.
3. One vegetable at least—carrot sticks, cucumber sticks, celery, radishes (except for a breakfast hike and even then you might like a ripe banana). The "walking salad" is good here.
4. Fruit — oranges, apples, peaches, pears (good thirst quenchers), dried raisins.
5. Enriched bread—in sandwiches or as bread and butter if you have a hard-cooked egg (carried in the shell) or chunk of cheese for number 1. Cookies and cake of enriched flour fit here too.

HAYBOX (HAY HOLE)

You can cut down on the time spent watching food cook, save fuel, and yet insure a hot meal on returning to the camp site after a long hike by using a haybox. See Chapter 12 for cooking in a hay hole.

Preparing the Haybox

1. Select a pot with a tight-fitting lid.

2. Dig a hole 1 ft. deeper and 1 ft. wider than the pot.
3. Line the hole with straw or hay and pack it down tightly until there is a layer of about 6 in. deep on the bottom.
4. Place the pot in the center of the hole and pack sides as tightly as possible.
5. Fill an old sack or cushion with hay or straw to a depth of 6 in. thick when pressed down. This is used to cover the hay hole.
6. When cooking, cover the hay hole with an old piece of canvas to prevent the heat from escaping. Weigh down with stones at the edge.
7. Erect a simple railing of sticks and twine to prevent people from stepping into it when not in use.

Prepare food for a haybox in the usual manner. Put it in a pot and bring to a rapid boil before placing it in the hay hole, then cover the pot quickly with a cushion and old canvas. Leave the food in the hay hole until the meal is to be served. Remove it and if necessary put it back on the fire for a few minutes before serving.

It takes at least three times as long to cook anything in a hay hole as on an ordinary fire, but no one has to stand by to watch it. Insulation in a large container will make a permanent haybox to be used where digging a hole is impossible. A portable haybox will keep food warm at the table, and food can be served right from the box. Ice cream as well as hot food can be made in a hay hole (see Chapter 12).

SANDWICHES

Sandwich menus are the most simple to prepare for all types of outings. You can plan a complete meal around a hearty sandwich combination or select a sandwich filling to go with

27

a hot dish. Suggestions for sandwich fillings appear on page 29. Pick one of these or make up one of your own.

In preparing sandwiches for an outing, use one-day-old bread—either sliced loaf or sliced rolls. Wheat, whole wheat, rye, raisin, bran, date or nut breads may be used. Cream the butter so it will spread easily and not tear the bread. For most sandwiches use one buttered and one unbuttered slice. Spread alternate faces so that the slices will fit when you are preparing a large number of sandwiches on a table at the same time.

A filling should be carefully seasoned and spread evenly and fully. One cup of filling usually is enough for four or five sandwiches.

Sandwiches are better if they are prepared as near serving time as possible. If they must be kept for some time, wrap them in a damp cloth and put them in a cool place. For packing they are kept fresh by wrapping in wax paper or other wrappings that are moisture proof.

Frozen sandwiches are handy where you can pack your "nosebag" from a freezer. They will be thawed for lunch at noon if taken from the freezer three hours before. Choose your fillings carefully for frozen sandwiches—meats, fish, poultry, cheese, and peanut butter are fine. These sandwiches will keep ten days to two weeks, so you can make a big batch ahead of time for day camp lunches, etc.

Sweet spreads such as honey, jelly, and preserves soak into the bread when used alone but not if butter, margarine, creamed cheese, etc., are spread to the edges on each slice first. Egg white toughens, mayonnaise separates, lettuce, tomato and other raw vegetables go limp when frozen, so they are not good for frozen sandwiches. Wrap each sandwich separately in moistureproof paper or foil, etc., before freezing and label as to contents. Never try to refreeze a thawed sandwich.

POTATO AND FRANKFURTER

12 frankfurters
1 pt. French dressing
12 medium-sized cold-cooked potatoes, diced
1 onion, peeled and minced
¼ C. chopped parsley
1 C. diced celery
10 medium-sized tomatoes, sliced

1. Prick the frankfurters well and cook them in boiling water to cover, or steam them until tender.
2. Then drain, skin them if necessary, and cut in thirds crosswise.
3. Chill well, add 1 C. of French dressing, and let stand for ½ hour.
4. Combine the diced potatoes, minced onion, chopped parsley, and diced celery.
5. Add enough well-seasoned French dressing to moisten well.
6. Chill thoroughly; then heap in a mound in the center of a cold platter.
7. Arrange the frankfurters around the potato salad, and then group thin slices of tomato, which have been sprinkled with salt and pepper, at the ends of platter.

SANDWICH FILLINGS

(Use 1 C. of filling for 4 to 5 sandwiches)

1. Chopped raisins or other dried fruits mixed with cream cheese, cottage cheese, or mayonnaise.
2. Peanut butter moistened with salad dressing and mixed with raisins, bananas, figs, dates, celery, olives, marmalade, cut marshmallows, jam or tomato catsup spread on bread with crisp lettuce.
3. Cream or cottage cheese mixed with shredded pineapple or raisins and chopped nuts—on Boston brown bread.
4. Cream or cottage cheese mixed with chopped, stuffed olives and mayonnaise dressing.
5. Tuna fish mixed with parsley, lemon juice, other seasonings and onions.

6. Chopped hard-cooked eggs, chopped ham or bacon, salt, pepper, mayonnaise.

7. Mashed sardines with equal amount of hard-cooked chopped eggs seasoned with salt, lemon juice and melted butter or margarine.

8. Bananas, lemon juice, brown or maple sugar, chopped nuts on whole wheat bread.

9. Grated American cheese, mixed with peppers, chopped stuffed olives and mayonnaise.

10. Grated Swiss cheese, chopped nuts, mayonnaise on rye bread.

11. To a ½ lb. of cottage cheese add 4 Tbsp. of chili sauce and a dash of Worcestershire sauce. Mixed olives may be added. Spread on buttered whole wheat bread.

12. To 4 Tbsp. creamed butter add ½ C. flaked sardines, 2 Tbsp. tomato catsup, 1 Tbsp. lemon juice, and 6 chopped olives. Spread on crisp whole wheat crackers. Tuna fish or salmon may be used in place of sardines.

13. Cream ½ lb. cream cheese and 2 Tbsp. of butter. Add ¼ C. orange juice, ½ C. chopped pimentos, 1 C. chopped nuts and ½ tsp. of salt. Spread between slices of buttered whole wheat or oatmeal bread.

14. Mix honey and chopped nuts and spread on buttered bread.

15. Chop 3 boiled, skinned frankfurters; mix with 3 Tbsp. of mayonnaise and ¼ tsp. prepared mustard.

16. Add 1 Tbsp. chili sauce and ¼ tsp. salt to ¼ C. firm mayonnaise. To this add 3 hard-cooked eggs chopped. Spread on buttered slices of white or whole wheat bread.

17. Mix ½ C. chopped nuts, ½ C. grated carrots, ½ tsp. salt, 1½ Tbsp. salad oil and 1 tsp. lemon juice.

18. Cream ¼ lb. butter or margarine; add 3 Tbsp. sugar and 1½ tsp. cinnamon. Spread on slices of bread. Also good toasted.

19. Chop very fine ½ lb. dried beef mixed with ¼ lb. grated American cheese; add 1 pt. tomatoes and cook until thick. When cold, serve as a filling for white bread sandwiches. A lettuce leaf in each sandwich is a good addition.

20. Wash and slice apples; rub slices with lemon juice to prevent apples from turning brown. Spread slices with: cream cheese and nuts, cream cheese and chopped red and green peppers, cream cheese and olives. Two slices of apples with cream cheese filling may be wrapped in wax paper or if the slices of apple are kept together the filling may be spread between the slices and the entire apple wrapped in waxed paper. This may serve as a salad or dessert for "nosebag" lunches (see pages 25-26).

RAW VEGETABLE COMBINATIONS

1. Shredded cabbage, diced apple, shredded coconut, French dressing, lettuce.
2. Cooked or canned green peas, diced cooked or canned beets, shredded cabbage, mayonnaise.
3. Sliced tomatoes, lettuce, grated cheese and nuts, French dressing.
4. Sliced cucumbers, chopped parsley, lettuce, French dressing.
5. Shredded cabbage, grated pineapple, shredded coconut, and sour cream dressing.
6. Shredded cabbage and Thousand Island dressing.
7. Shredded cabbage, chopped peanuts, and boiled dressing.
8. Sliced and quartered tomatoes arranged on shredded cabbage, served with mayonnaise.
9. Shredded cabbage, diced cooked beets, horseradish with sweetened vinegar. This is a good combination with baked beans.

10. Shredded cabbage, grated raw carrots, onions chopped fine, boiled dressing.
11. Shredded cabbage, dates, nuts, with sour cream dressing.
12. Shredded cabbage, chopped cucumber pickle, diced celery, diced hard-cooked eggs, dressing.
13. Shredded cabbage, watercress, raisins, French dressing.
14. Diced unpeeled apples, grated parsnips, French dressing (made with lemon juice).
15. Shredded cabbage, oranges, sour cream dressing.
16. Cucumber, lettuce, chopped nuts, sour cream dressing.
17. Shredded cabbage, diced pimento, diced apples, chopped nutmeats, lettuce, and mayonnaise.
18. Shredded cabbage, grated cheese, green peppers, French dressing.
19. Avocado slices and grapefruit sections with French dressing on lettuce. Use the grapefruit juice instead of vinegar in the dressing.

WALDORF SALAD

4 apples, diced
1 bunch celery, diced
1 C. nutmeats
lettuce
1 C. mayonnaise

1. Mix equal parts of apple and celery and moisten with mayonnaise.
2. Garnish with nuts or strips of green peppers and pimentos.
3. Serve on lettuce leaf or other greens.

In apple season, an attractive way to serve this salad is to hollow out red apples, fill the cavity with the salad, and top with dressing.

SPINACH AND ORANGE

½ lb. young spinach
1 C. French dressing
8 oranges

1. Arrange slices of orange on crisp, washed spinach leaves.
2. Serve with French dressing.

WALKING SALAD

12 apples
2 C. cottage cheese
½ C. raisins
½ C. nuts
2 Tbsp. mayonnaise

1. Cut the tops off the apples and core them, leaving the bottom skin over the hole.
2. Scoop out the pulp of apples and chop with cheese, raisins and nuts.
3. Mix with mayonnaise.
4. Stuff the mixture into the apple shells and put the tops on.

This salad is called Walking Salad because it can be eaten while hiking.

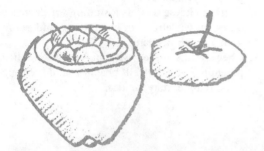

TOSSED SALAD

1 bunch celery
1 cabbage head or other green vegetable
1 head lettuce
1 cucumber
salt, pepper
1 C. French dressing

1. Chop celery, cabbage, lettuce and cucumber.
2. Season to taste.
3. Just before serving toss the salad with French dressing.
4. Serve immediately.

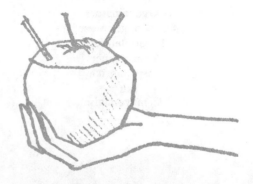

33

MINT AND SORREL LEAF WAFERS

mint and sorrel leaves
1 egg white, beaten stiffly
¼ C. sugar

1. Gather mint and sorrel leaves.
2. Beat egg whites stiffly.
3. Dip the leaves in egg white and then in the sugar.
4. Place on a platter or flat surface and let the "leaf wafers" dry.
5. Serve at woodland tea.

Dry weather is better than damp weather for this recipe.

BIRD'S NEST

6 large tomatoes
4 C. cottage cheese
2 heads lettuce
¼ tsp. pepper
½ tsp. paprika
salt
1 C. mayonnaise

1. Cut tomatoes in half and remove the pulp.
2. Season the cottage cheese with pepper, paprika, and salt, if not already salted sufficiently.
3. Chill and form into balls the size of large marbles.
4. Put 3 balls into each tomato half and serve on lettuce or watercress.
5. Mix tomato pulp with mayonnaise and use as dressing.

COTTAGE CHEESE COMBINATIONS

1. Cottage cheese, diced apple, diced celery, lettuce, mayonnaise.
2. Cheese balls rolled in chopped nutmeats, apples, mayonnaise.
3. Cottage cheese used as a stuffing for prunes or dates, nuts, lettuce or watercress and served with French dressing.
4. Cheese balls served with halved pears, sliced pineapple, or halved peaches and chopped nuts, lettuce, mayonnaise.

CHEESE BALLS AND WATERCRESS

4 C. cottage cheese
1 C. chopped nuts
¾ tsp. paprika
2 tsp. salt
⅓ C. tomato catsup
2 bunches watercress
¾ C. mayonnaise

1. The cottage cheese should be dry and unsalted.
2. Mix cheese with the catsup, salt, paprika, and salted nuts.
3. Chill thoroughly and form into small balls.
4. Place 3 or 4 balls on a bed of crisp watercress and serve cold with mayonnaise.

CELERY STICKS

2 bunches celery
2 or 3 (8 oz.) pkgs. soft yellow cheese

1. Clean celery and stuff each stalk with cheese. This may be varied by stuffing stalks with peanut butter.

BUNNY

2 heads lettuce
3 C. cottage cheese
1 C. seedless raisins
1 C. chopped nutmeats
1 C. mayonnaise
salt

1. Mix together the cottage cheese, raisins, and nuts.
2. Add the mayonnaise and blend thoroughly; add salt if needed.
3. Using the large outer leaves of crisp lettuce, spread them with the cheese mixture and roll up like a jelly roll. (The recipe will make about 24 rolls.)
4. In season, tie each roll with a long-stemmed nasturtium. Place 2 rolls on each plate with the flowers on top and some of the tiny leaves of lettuce between. Clover blossoms may also be used, but the rolls will stay together without any tying. Strips of pimento around each roll may be used if they are not tied.

APPLE, CHEESE, AND WATERCRESS

6 large apples
¾ lb. cream or cottage cheese
watercress
currant jelly
1 C. French dressing

1. Wash and core apples, leaving the skins on, and cut crosswise into inch-thick slices.
2. Mix the jelly with cheese until a smooth paste is formed.
3. Spread this mixture on the slices of apples.
4. Mix watercress with French dressing.
5. Lay greens on one side of the plate and the apple slices on the other.

ASPARAGUS AND EGG

3 (1 lb., 4 oz.) cans asparagus
1 head lettuce
6 eggs (hard-cooked)
salt
strips of pimento or green pepper
1 C. French dressing

1. Arrange canned (or fresh cooked) asparagus stalks on lettuce leaf or other salad greens, with the stalks parallel and the heads together.
2. Arrange sliced eggs on asparagus.
3. Season with salt.
4. Serve with French dressing.
   Strip of green pepper or pimento may be used for additional color, or the asparagus stalks may be placed through the green pepper ring.

ORANGE AND DATE

1 lb. dates
¼ lb. pimento cheese
1 C. chopped nuts
watercress (or lettuce)
lemon or orange juice
6 oranges
1 C. French dressing

1. Clean and remove stones from dates.
2. Combine the pimento cheese and chopped nuts and fill the dates.
3. Roll dates in either lemon or orange juice.

36

4. Peel the oranges carefully, divide into sections, and place alternately with the dates on the watercress.
5. Serve with French dressing.

Stewed prunes and celery may be used in place of the dates and nuts.

CARROT AND APPLE

4 C. thinly sliced apple
1 C. mayonnaise
4 C. grated carrot
lettuce

1. Cut the apple into very thin slices.
2. Arrange apple slices on lettuce.
3. Spread with mayonnaise and sprinkle grated carrot on top. Place more dressing in center.

ITALIAN SALAD

2 heads shredded lettuce
1 bunch celery, diced
8 tomatoes, cut in quarters
1 can anchovies, diced
salt, pepper
¾ lb. salami, diced
½ lb. Italian firm cheese, diced
½ C. salad oil
¼ C. vinegar

1. Toss ingredients in a dressing made of ½ C. of salad oil and ¼ C. of vinegar.

FRENCH DRESSING

1 lemon (juice)
4 tsp. honey
salt
cayenne
mustard
vegetable oil

1. Put lemon juice, honey, a little salt, cayenne, and a bit of mustard into a 16 oz. (1 pt.) bottle.
2. Shake vigorously till all ingredients are thoroughly mixed; then add small amounts of vegetable or olive oil, shaking thoroughly after each addition until the bottle is half full.

This dressing should stay mixed for some time without separating.

COLE SLAW

1 large hard cabbage
6 slices pineapple
2 C. raisins
½ pt. mayonnaise

1. Shred cabbage.
2. Cut up pineapple.
3. Add raisins.
4. Mix with mayonnaise before serving. Season to taste.

Celery, cheese, green peas, carrots, or other vegetables may be used with the cabbage for variation.

LETTUCE DRESSING

1 C. mixed vegetables, including: radishes, cucumbers, green peppers, parsley.
pimentoes
olives
lemon juice
horseradish
1 C. mayonnaise

1. Chop vegetables fine.
2. Mix well with lemon juice and mayonnaise.
3. Add horseradish.
4. Use on head lettuce or other salad greens.

THOUSAND ISLAND DRESSING

1 hard-cooked egg, chopped
1 Tbsp. chopped onion
1 Tbsp. chopped green pepper
2 tsp. chopped pimento
2 Tbsp. chili sauce
2 Tbsp. catsup
½ tsp. salt
¼ tsp. paprika
¾ C. mayonnaise

1. Mix ingredients.
2. Chill and serve.
   Good with lettuce and hard-cooked eggs.

PARSLEY DRESSING

1 C. French dressing
parsley (small amount), chopped
1 Tbsp. green onion tops, chopped fine

1. Add parsley and green onion tops to French dressing.
2. Serve with vegetable salads.

SOUR CREAM SALAD DRESSING

1 C. sour cream
1 lemon
½ C. sugar

1. Whip cream until stiff.
2. For fruit salads add sugar and lemon juice to taste. When used with vegetables, season with salt and a dash of pepper.

BANANA AND MINT

12 bananas
3 Tbsp. lemon juice
5 Tbsp. chopped mint
¾ C. chopped nuts
1¼ C. mayonnaise
lettuce

1. Remove skins from bananas and cut them in halves, lengthwise.
2. Place on beds of crisp lettuce and sprinkle with lemon juice and chopped mint.
3. Garnish with the mayonnaise and nuts combined.

39

PRUNE WHIP

1½ lbs. dried prunes
6 Tbsp. lemon juice
6 Tbsp. sugar
1½ C. walnut meats, finely chopped

1. Stew dried prunes until they are soft and tender.
2. Remove stones.
3. Whip prunes with lemon juice, sugar, and nuts.
4. Chill thoroughly and serve.

BANANA WHIP

12 ripe bananas
¼ C. lemon juice
¼ C. sugar
1 C. finely chopped walnut meats

1. Mash bananas until smooth.
2. Add lemon juice, sugar, and nuts.
3. Chill thoroughly and serve.

To vary the flavor, add two teaspoons of finely chopped mint to the bananas before chilling them.

BIRCHERMUESLI Switzerland

¾ C. oatmeal flakes
(or 1 Tbsp. per person)
¾ C. condensed milk or yogurt
¼ C. lemon juice
3 C. fruits—bananas, oranges,
plums, peaches, grated apple, currants.

1. Mix the oatmeal (uncooked), condensed milk, lemon.
2. Add fruits.
3. Mix and chill. Add nuts if desired.

This dish can be served at breakfast, as a dessert, and as a snack.

FRUIT BALLS

Dried fruits:
figs, apricots, dates, raisins, prunes, nutmeats, honey, grated coconut.

1. Chop and mix the dried fruits and nutmeats.
2. Moisten with enough honey to make the fruits stick together.
3. Form into balls.
4. Roll in coconut.

FROZEN GRAHAM CRACKER PUDDING
(Hay Hole Ice Cream)

This recipe calls for the hay hole method of freezing as described in Chapter 12.

⅓ C. sugar
1½ C. evaporated milk
¾ C. water
3 tsp. vanilla
¾ C. graham cracker crumbs

1. Mix together sugar, evaporated milk, water, and vanilla. Add cracker crumbs last.
2. Put in tightly covered freezer can.
3. Set this can in packed ice (8 parts crushed ice to 1 part ice cream salt) or dry ice. (Avoid handling dry ice with bare hands.) The ice may be packed around the freezer can in the hay hole (or in a second container holding the ice and freezer can which can then be put into the hay hole).

Makes about 1 qt. which serves 6 to 8 persons. Allow 3 to 4 hours for freezing.

MALLOW SQUARES

2¾ C. (½ lb.) graham cracker crumbs
1 C. (½ lb.) sliced dates
1 qt. (½ lb.) marshmallows cut in eighths
1 C. chopped nuts
1 C. evaporated milk

1. Spread ½ C. of crumbs on bottom of pans.
2. Mix remaining crumbs, dates, marshmallows, and nuts together.
3. Blend milk into mixture.
4. Divide into equal parts for each pan.
5. Roll in crumbs; then press mixture down to fit pan.
6. Chill before cutting into pieces approximately 1½ in. square.

Makes 36 squares and fills two 9x9x1½ in. pans.

Miniature marshmallows are now available and may be used in place of large ones since they do not have to be cut.

DRIED FRUIT

24 halves dried apricots or other dried fruits
½ C. mayonnaise
1 C. chopped nutmeats
1 C. raisins

1. Wash the fruit well and soak until tender.
2. Cool and roll in chopped nuts.
3. Fill the center with raisins and nuts and serve on lettuce leaf or other garnish.

Variation

1 lb. prunes
1 lb. dates
1 lb. raisins
½ lb. cottage cheese
1 pkg. shredded coconut
¼ lb. nutmeats
1 C. dressing
lettuce

For each serving use 2 prunes, 2 dates, and about 2 Tbsp. of raisins.

1. Soak the prunes in cold water (and/or cook) until tender.
2. Remove stones from prunes and dates.
3. Stuff prunes with cottage cheese and dates with walnut meats.
4. Chop raisins, make into balls, and roll in coconut.
5. Arrange the fruit on lettuce.
6. Serve with mayonnaise or French dressing.

DRIED MILK FOR DRINKING

4 C. powdered milk
4 qts. water

1. Add powdered milk slowly to water at room temperature, beating continuously while combining. Dissolve any lumps.
2. Let milk stand in cold place before using. Flavor if desired.

If richer milk is desired, use ⅓ to ½ less water. The more concentrated product resembles cream. Dried milk may be used for cooking and as a beverage. Follow directions on package.

ORANGEADE

1 C. sugar
1 C. orange juice
(approximately 2-4 oranges)
1 C. water
2½ qts. water
grated rind of one orange

1. Boil 1 C. of sugar and 1 C. of water for 5 minutes.
2. Add juice, grated rind, and 2½ qts. of water.
3. Serve cold.

EVAPORATED MILK FOR DRINKING

4 tall cans (14 oz.) evaporated milk
7 C. water

1. Measure milk and water into a pitcher and stir until thoroughly mixed or shake in a glass fruit jar.
2. Chill before serving as a beverage.

This milk may also be used in cooking and as a milk base for other beverages.

EGG NOG

3 qts. milk (cold)
1 tsp. salt
10 eggs
1 Tbsp. vanilla
6 Tbsp. sugar (if desired)

1. Beat eggs thoroughly.
2. Add salt, sugar, vanilla, and milk.
3. Mix well; serve cold.

LEMONADE

1 C. sugar
1 C. lemon juice
(approximately 6 lemons)
1 C. water
2½ qts. water
grated rind of 1 lemon

1. Boil 1 C. of water and 1 C. of sugar for 5 minutes.
2. Add lemon juice, grated rind, and 2½ quarts of water.
3. Chill and serve.

FRUIT MILK SHAKE

6 C. grape, pineapple, or berry juice
8 C. milk

1. Mix milk and juice and shake together in a glass fruit jar.
2. If juice is tart, sugar may be added.

FRUIT PUNCH (POWDERED)

Dehydrated fruit flavors come in various assortments, and the instructions for using these products are on the packages. On trail hikes and pack trips these fruit flavors are lightweight and easily packed and lend variety to the camp beverage.

9. KETTLE AND SKILLET COOKING

Skillets and kettles can be set over fires of softwoods, hardwoods, or charcoal. Just be sure you have coated the *outside* of the pot with soap or other detergent, since newly lighted fires are frequently smoky, and resin in woods makes a sticky coating that is hard to remove from utensils unless there is an undercoating of detergent.

You need to hold the kettle above the fire. It can rest on a grate (or grill) of a stone or brick fireplace (see page 57); on a charcoal brazier (see page 133); on the sides of a trench fire (see page 64); on the two large green logs of the hunter's fire (see page 68); or on strategically located rocks (not shale) at a camp site. In addition, if the kettle has a bail, it can be held by cranes and pot hooks (see pages 60 and 63).

The fire can be the one you prefer (see Chapter 4). Before you go out to cook a meal over a fire, practice your fire building and test yourself and your friends. Have each one build and light a fire under a small kettle of water (one cup) to see whose fire will boil the water first. Suspend these kettles an equal distance above each of the fires so you will all start together with the same handicap.

In laying your fire note from what direction the wind is blowing. Lay a Basic A fire with the open end of the V to the wind. Light this

BASIC A FIRE

45

fire or the Tepee one with your back to the wind. Light the fire near the bottom so the flames have tinder and kindling to reach for above. Be sure there is enough air space for draft to bring plenty of oxygen needed by the fire. This applies when adding more fuel in the log cabin fashion. Have the kettles on or above the fire when you light it to get every bit of heat from that fire. Follow the directions in Chapter 4 for safety in fire building. See illustrations of fires on pages 12 and 45.

You'll discover in the recipes in this chapter that the foods come from all over the world and include meat, fish, eggs, cheese, and vegetable dishes. There are recipes to eat for breakfast, lunch, dinner, and even for dessert; for quick breads and fritters fried in deep fat or steamed over the fire; for various beverages and desserts; and for candies. Read them carefully to find those recipes that are designed to meet your requirements of ingredients, time, type of fire, and menu.

BREAD GRIDDLE CAKES

2 C. fine bread crumbs (or 2 C. of
any cold cereal, crushed)
4 eggs
1 C. flour
1 tsp. salt
7 tsp. baking powder

1. Mix in the order given.
2. Fry on a griddle or tin-can stove.

HONEY BUTTER

½ lb. butter or margarine
1 pt. honey

1. Cream butter.
2. Warm honey and beat until clear and creamy.
3. Combine butter and honey and beat until well mixed.

The quantities may be varied according to taste; that is, more butter and less honey or vice versa. This makes a delicious spread for hot griddle cakes, French toast, muffins, or plain toast.

FLAPJACKS
(Pancakes, Flannel Cakes or Griddle Cakes)

5 C. flour
3½ Tbsp. baking powder
1 Tbsp. salt
6 Tbsp. sugar
4 eggs
2 C. Milk

1. Mix dry ingredients.
2. Add liquids only when the fire has burned down to coals. The batter should be just thick enough to pour from a spoon.
3. Heat a pan and grease it thoroughly but with no extra grease. The pan should be level to insure even baking.
4. Pour in enough batter to cover the bottom of the pan completely.
5. When the top of the batter is covered with bubbles and the edges are crisp, loosen the cake from the bottom by shaking the pan.
6. Flip the cake over and cook on the other side.

47

FRENCH TOAST

1½ C. milk
½ tsp. salt
6 eggs
24 slices of bread

1. Beat eggs and add milk and salt.
2. Dip slices of bread in the egg mixture until entirely covered.
3. Fry in butter or other shortening and brown on both sides.

HOMINY

Hominy is made by boiling ripe green corn with hardwood ashes, preferably of hickory, until the grains slip from the hulls. Then the hulls are washed away and the hulled corn washed in several waters until all the lye is removed. This hominy may then be prepared in several ways.

The Indians sometimes made hominy into soup, either with plain water or with meat stock. It was also boiled whole by itself or cooked and served together with meat. Sometimes it was mashed into a paste and in that form made into a porridge.

Hominy paste was also made into dumplings, either plain or with boiled beans mixed with it. A lump of fat for seasoning was placed in the center of each dumpling. Any dumplings left over at one meal were drained of the water in which they had been cooked and were mashed and fried for another meal.

CEREALS

(Oatmeal, Wheat, Corn)

Follow directions on package. Use milk instead of water; mix dry milk with dry raw cereal and add to water.

HUSH PUPPIES   Southeastern United States

4 C. cornmeal
¼ C. flour
2 C. milk
4 eggs
4 tsp. baking powder
1 medium-sized onion
1 Tbsp. salt

1 Mix flour, cornmeal, baking powder, and salt together.
2. Add milk and well-beaten eggs.
3. Grate onion. Add to mixture. This should form a rather stiff mixture—stiff enough to shape into balls.
4. Drop from a spoon into hot, deep fat, and cook at moderate speed until the balls are a golden brown.
5. Balls about ½-2 in. in diameter are a nice size. (They may be cooked in the fat used to fry fish and are served with fried fish.)

TORTILLAS Mexico

This is a Mexican bread sometimes served with chili con carne or enchiladas.

2½ C. cornmeal
2 C. flour
1 Tbsp. baking powder
¾ tsp. salt
1½ Tbsp. shortening
1¼ C. milk

1. Mix the dry ingredients and rub in the shortening with fingers or cut in with pastry blender or 2 knives.
2. Stir in the milk.
3. Flour the board.
4. Pat and roll out pieces of dough about the size of an egg until the edges are very thin.
5. Put a little fat in the frying pan and cook the cakes until they are a delicate brown.
6. Turn and brown on the other side.
7. Butter and serve hot with or without preserves.

49

DOUBLE BOILER BREAD

8 tsp. baking powder
1¼ tsp. salt
3 C. flour
¾ C. yellow cornmeal
3 Tbsp. sugar
1 C. chopped dates
4 tsp. caraway seeds
2 C. milk
2 Tbsp. melted shortening

1. Mix the salt and baking powder with the flour.
2. Add cornmeal, sugar, dates, and caraway seeds, stirring the whole into the milk (preferably warm milk).
3. Add the shortening.
4. Grease thickly the inside of a double boiler. Then shake a spoonful of flour around in it until the grease is evenly coated. Shake out all that will not adhere.
5. Pour in the batter and cook over hot water for 1 hour or until bread is firm. It may require longer cooking, but it will not be spoiled by overcooking.
6. Turn out on a dish and serve, hot or cold, in buttered slices.

SPIDER CORN BREAD
Northwestern United States

4 eggs
2 C. milk
2 tsp. baking powder
2 C. cornmeal
1 tsp. salt
2 Tbsp. fat

1. Beat eggs.
2. Add milk, cornmeal, salt, baking powder, and melted fat and mix.
3. Pour mixture into a hot greased heavy iron frying pan, cover, and cook over flame.
4. When half done, turn.

Makes enough for 2 cakes of corn bread.

SCRAMBLED EGGS AND CORN

2 (1 lb., 13 oz.) cans corn (drained) or
6 ears cooked corn
2 Tbsp. butter or margarine
2 tsp. salt
¼ tsp. pepper
8 eggs, beaten

1. Cut the corn from the cob or drain canned corn.
2. Melt butter in a frying pan, add corn, and season to taste.
3. When well heated, add the beaten eggs.
4. Stir and scrape carefully from the bottom of pan and cook gently until eggs are set.

CALIFORNIA EGG CRACKLE

1 lb. bacon
12 eggs
½ C. milk
salt, pepper
¾ C. cheese cracker crumbs

1. Fry diced bacon; drain excess grease.
2. Add milk and well-beaten eggs.
3. Season with salt and pepper.
4. Stir constantly. Just before eggs become completely dry, add crushed cheese crackers.

CREAMED EGGS

½ C. butter or margarine
½ C. flour
4 C. milk
12 hard-boiled eggs, sliced
1 can pimentos, diced
salt, pepper, paprika
24 slices toast

1. Melt butter; add flour and cook until bubbling.
2. Add milk gradually, stirring constantly, and cook until smooth and thick.
3. Add sliced eggs and diced pimento.
4. Season and serve on toast.
5. Sprinkle top with paprika.

Undiluted, concentrated cream of **mushroom**, celery, or chicken soup may be used for white sauce.

51

VENETIAN EGGS

½ lb. salt pork, diced
3 medium onions, diced
2 (1 lb., 13 oz.) cans tomatoes
1½ C. bread or cracker crumbs
1½ lb. American cheese
salt, pepper
5 eggs
toast or crackers

1. Fry salt pork, and onions.
2. Add the tomatoes and crumbs to fried onions and seasoning. Cook until thick.
3. Break cheese into small pieces and stir it in quickly so that it melts but does not become stringy.
4. Break eggs into the mixture after removing it from the fire.
5. Stir briskly and serve on toast or crackers.

BEET BORSCH

6 large beets
2 onions
2 qts. water
1¼ tsp. salt
2 tsp. sugar
2 egg yolks
2 C. milk
¼ C. lemon juice

1. Cut beets in strips and cook in water with chopped onion, salt, and sugar until soft.
2. While still warm, add slowly a mixture of well-beaten egg yolks and milk to thicken.
3. Flavor with lemon juice.
4. May be served hot or cold. Cabbage and tomato combined, beet greens, or spinach may be used instead of beets.

KALA MOJAKKAA   Finland
(Fish Chowder)

1 large northern pike or similar fish
cut into suitable pieces for serving
2 qts. boiling water
salt
15 whole peppercorns
12 potatoes, diced
2 C. celery, diced
2 large onions, diced
6 carrots, diced
1 qt. whole milk
1 C. (or less) butter or margarine

1. Cook the fish for about 10 minutes in seasoned water.
2. Remove the fish, cool, and bone it
3. To the same water add the diced vegetables and cook until tender.
4. Add milk, butter, and fish.
5. Heat to boiling point and serve. If less liquid is desired, drain off some of the water before adding the milk.

FRENCH ONION SOUP

8 large onions
½ C. vegetable oil (or meat drippings)
3 qts. water
salt, pepper
8 slices of stale bread, toasted
½ lb. grated Swiss or American brick cheese

1. Peel onions and slice very thin.
2. Fry them slowly in fat until a uniform golden brown, using a kettle deep enough to hold the water to be added next.
3. When onions are thoroughly fried add the hot water. The onions will make a clean brown liquor without use of meat. Soup stock may be used instead of water, or beef extract or bouillon cubes may be added to the water if a meat soup is preferred.
4. Cover and let simmer ¾ of an hour, seasoning to taste.
5. Put in soup dishes.
6. Add triangles of toast and sprinkle with cheese.

53

CORN CHOWDER

12 slices fat bacon or salt pork
6 onions
10 medium-sized potatoes, diced
2 (1 lb. 13 oz.) cans or 5 C. corn
salt and pepper
2 qts. liquid (water, stock, or milk)

1. Cut bacon or pork and onions very small.
2. Fry in a kettle until brown, stirring frequently to prevent burning. Pour off extra grease, if necessary.
3. Add diced potatoes about ½ hour before time for serving and cook until done.
4. Just before potatoes are done, add corn.
5. Season and add liquid. If milk is used, add just prior to serving.
6. Bring to a boiling point, but do not boil.

Variations

This is a basic chowder recipe that may be varied as desired. Ham, fish, clams or other vegetables may be used in place of the corn. If meat, fish, or raw vegetables are used instead of corn, it will be necessary to cook them longer.

Ham Chowder—use 5 C. of cubed ham instead of corn.

Fish Chowder—use 5 or 6 C. of fish in place of corn or ham.

Carrot Chowder—5 C. of diced carrots may be substituted for corn, ham, or fish.

Celery Chowder—8 C. of finely diced celery may be used in place of corn, ham, fish, or carrots. Just before serving, add 5 chopped hard-boiled eggs.

FRUKT SUPPE   Norway
(Fruit Soup)

1 lb. prunes
2 apples, diced
1 C. raisins
2 sticks cinnamon or 2 tsp. cinnamon
½ C. minute tapioca
1 qt. raspberries or other such fruit
1 qt. canned blueberries

1. Boil the prunes, diced apples, raisins, and cinnamon in enough water to cover.
2. When fruit is almost tender, add tapioca and cook until tapioca is transparent.
3. Add berries.
4. Serve hot as first course or chilled as dessert.

NEW ENGLAND CHOWDER
1 qt. clams
5 C. potatoes, raw and cubed
2 in. cube fat pork
2 onions, sliced
flour
1¼ Tbsp. salt
¼ tsp. pepper
⅓ C. butter or margarine
6 C. scalded milk
12 common or Boston crackers

1. Using 1 C. water, clean and pick clams.
2. Save this water from clams, strain, heat to boiling point and set aside.
3. Chop finely the hard part of the clams.
4. Cut pork into small pieces and fry.
5. Add sliced onions and fry for 5 minutes.
6. Strain off the grease.
7. Cover the potatoes with boiling water and parboil for only 5 minutes.
8. Drain and add a layer of potatoes over pork and onions in kettle.
9. Add chopped clams, sprinkle with salt and pepper, and dredge generously with flour.
10. Add remaining potatoes. Again sprinkle with salt and pepper, dredge with flour, and add 3 C. boiling water.
11. Cook 10 minutes.
12. Add milk, soft part of clams, ⅓ C. butter (save 1 Tbsp. for later) and boil 3 minutes.
13. Add crackers split in half.
14. Reheat clam water, thicken with extra Tbsp. butter and 1 Tbsp. flour cooked together.
15. Add to chowder just before serving. (Clam water may cause milk to separate so it is added last.)

Fish, corn, or carrots may be substituted for clams in this chowder.

55

SHREDDED CABBAGE

2 small heads cabbage
⅛ lb. butter or margarine
salt, pepper, paprika

1. Shred the cabbage and cook for 15-20 minutes in 3 C. of boiling salted water in covered kettle.
2. Remove and drain liquid from cabbage.
3. Pour melted butter over top, sprinkle with paprika, and serve hot.

SALMON WIGGLE

3 (1 lb.) cans salmon
2 (1 lb., 4 oz.) cans peas
1 Tbsp. lemon juice
¼ C. fat
¼ C. flour
3 C. milk
1 tsp. salt
pepper
toast or crackers

1. Drain salmon and peas but save liquid to add to white sauce.
2. Flake salmon with a fork and season with lemon juice.
3. Prepare a white sauce with fat, flour, milk, and the liquid from peas and salmon.
4. Season with salt and pepper.
5. Add salmon and peas and heat thoroughly.
6. Serve on hot buttered toast or crackers.

DESERT FISH Southwestern United States

2 lbs. salt pork, diced
½ C. butter or margarine
½ C. flour
8 C. milk
12 slices toast

1. Fry salt pork until it is golden brown.
2. Pour over the crisp pork a white sauce that is made in the following way: Melt butter, add flour, and blend thoroughly. Add milk gradually, stirring constantly. Cook until smooth.
3. Serve desert fish on toast.

CHILI CON CARNE   Mexico

½ C. chopped onion
2½ lbs. ground steak or left-over meat
¼ C. bacon dripping
2 Tbsp. chili powder
2 C. canned tomatoes
salt
3 C. cooked kidney beans or 2 (15 oz.) cans

1. Fry onion in fat until light brown.
2. Add meat and cook until done.
3. Add tomatoes and beans and season with chili powder and salt. Let simmer, thickening with a little flour if needed.
4. Add 2 tablespoons of Worcestershire sauce if more seasoning is needed. Campers may not like too much seasoning.

SAUTÉ CHIPPED BEEF WITH BANANAS

1 lb. chipped beef
⅓ C. bacon fat
12 bananas
¼ C. flour

1. Heat the bacon fat in a frying pan.
2. Add the chipped beef which has been picked into small pieces.
3. Fry quickly for about 3 minutes or until heated through and slightly browned.
4. Arrange in the center of a hot platter and keep hot.
5. Then in the same fat, fry the bananas, which have been cut in halves crosswise and dusted with flour. Cook until golden brown.
6. Arrange around the beef and serve at once.

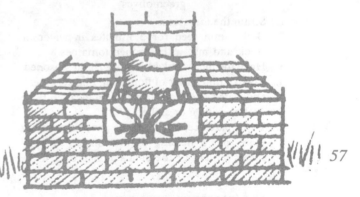

57

PERMANENT FIREPLACE

MEXICAN ENCHILADAS

2 (1 lb., 3 oz.) cans tomatoes
1 Tbsp. cumin seed
water
2½ lbs. cooked meat (any mixture;
chicken, ham, or veal are best)
2½ C. flour
1¼ tsp. salt
½ C. fine cornmeal
parsley
1 lb. grated cheese
green olives

1. Strain the tomatoes.
2. Boil cumin seed for 5 minutes in water or stock and mix with strained tomatoes.
3. Have the meat cooked, chopped, and seasoned.
4. Make a thin batter of flour, salt, fine cornmeal, and water, and make large thin pancakes. Bake on hot griddle or skillet.
5. Lay a pancake, hot from the pan, on each hot plate, put a helping of the mixed, chopped meats on half of the pancake, flap over it the other half, and pour on top a portion of the sauce.
6. Sprinkle pancakes with grated cheese and minced parsley.
7. Garnish with stoned and sliced green olives, and serve with crackers.

CREAMED CHIPPED BEEF

1½ lbs. chipped beef
½ C. butter or margarine
½ C. flour
5 C. milk
12 slices toast
or 12 baked or boiled potatoes
salt, pepper, paprika

1. Pick the chipped beef into small pieces and frizzle it in the butter.
2. Add flour and mix thoroughly.
3. Then add milk gradually, stirring constantly, and cook until smooth and thick.
4. Season; serve on toast or potatoes.
5. Garnish with paprika.

FAAR I KAAL Norway

(Lamb in Cabbage)

4 lbs. lamb shoulder, cut into pieces as for stew
2 medium heads cabbage
1 medium onion, diced
15 whole peppers
salt

1. Boil the meat in a deep kettle until partly done.
2. Add the whole peppers, salt, onion, and sectioned cabbage.
3. Boil until meat is tender and cabbage is done.

KARBONADE KAKER Norway

(Hamburger Patties)

2 lbs. hamburger
fat for frying
¼ tsp. nutmeg
salt, pepper

1. Season the hamburger, form into thin patties, and fry in skillet (or on a No. 10 tin can); or broil.
2. Place between sandwich buns.

KOMAC STEW

4 onions
½ C. butter or margarine
3 (1 lb. 3 oz.) cans tomatoes or
8 large fresh tomatoes
3 green peppers
salt, pepper
10 eggs
12 slices toast or crackers

1. Peel and slice onions.
2. Fry in hot melted butter until pale brown in the hot fat.
3. Add tomatoes (if ripe ones are used, peel and cut them up) and the green peppers that have been washed, seeded, and diced.
4. Cover and let the mixture stew slowly for ½ hour with frequent stirring.
5. Season to taste, and add the eggs, one by one, stirring all the time.
6. Serve at once on toast or crackers.

59

CAMPFIRE STEW

3 lbs. hamburger steak
1 large onion, peeled and diced
1 Tbsp. fat
3 (10 oz.) cans concentrated vegetable soup
salt, pepper

1. Make little balls of hamburger, adding seasoning.
2. Fry with onions in a frying pan or in the bottom of a kettle until onion is light brown and balls are well-browned all over.
3. Pour off excess fat.
4. Add vegetable soup and enough water or soup stock to prevent sticking.
5. Cover and cook slowly until meat balls are cooked all through. Serve hot.

LIHA MOJAKKAA   Finland
(Beef Stew)

2 lbs. beef, cubed
2 qts. water
salt, pepper
18 potatoes, quartered
2 onions, quartered
8 carrots, quartered

1. Parboil meat in the seasoned water.
2. Add vegetables and cook until tender.

KETTLE ON CRANE

ARROZ CON POLLO   Cuba, Mexico

5 lbs. frying chicken, cut up
1 C. butter or salad oil
2 C. finely chopped onion
1 C. chopped green pepper
2 cloves garlic, finely chopped
4 C. cooked tomatoes
½ C. tomato paste or chili sauce
1 C. water
4 bay leaves
3 tsp. salt
2 C. rice
2 tsp. vinegar
1 C. mushrooms, optional
2 C. cooked peas, optional

1. Heat butter or oil in heavy kettle.
2. Add chicken and brown.
3. Remove chicken and add onion, pepper, and garlic. Cook until lightly browned.
4. Add tomatoes, tomato paste, water, bay leaves, salt, and chicken. Cover and cook over low heat 40 minutes.
5. Stir in rice; cover and continue cooking over low heat. Stir again after 10 minutes.
6. Add vinegar, mushrooms, and peas; cook 10 minutes longer.
7. Serve on hot platter, with pieces of chicken around the rice.

SOUTHERN GOULASH

¼ C. fat
2 lbs. ground beef
2 onions, chopped fine
2 C. beef broth
2 tsp. salt
2½ C. uncooked spaghetti
2 C. hot water
2 tsp. Worcestershire sauce

1. Heat fat and sear beef and onions in it.
2. Add remaining ingredients.
3. Cover and cook on low heat 15 minutes and simmer 20 minutes (cook 35 minutes total).

61

AMERICAN GOULASH

4 small onions, peeled and diced
green pepper, if desired, cut small
1 Tbsp. fat
3 lbs. hamburger steak
4 16 oz. cans spaghetti and tomato sauce
salt, pepper

1. Fry onions and green pepper in fat until brown.
2. Pour off excess fat.
3. Add hamburger steak and cook until well done, but not crisply brown.
4. Add spaghetti and heat well.
5. Season to taste. Serve hot.

For variety, use one 1 lb. package of macaroni, instead of canned spaghetti, and one (10 oz.) can of concentrated tomato soup. Cook macaroni in boiling water. Takes an extra kettle.

A little sausage meat with the hamburger and cooked celery may also be used.

62

MULLIGAN STEW

1½ lbs. beef in pieces
1½ lbs. lamb in pieces
3 fistsful flour
3 qts. boiling water
1 in. sq. butter or margarine
3 carrots, thinly sliced
2 parsnips, thinly sliced
1 large onion, diced
2 green peppers, diced
2 sticks celery, diced
8 potatoes, diced
celery salt
salt, pepper, paprika

1. Wash, dry, season, and roll meat in 2 fistsful of flour.
2. Put butter and meat into a frying pan and sear the meat on both sides.
3. Put prepared vegetables in boiling water.
4. Add meat and simmer for about 2 hours.
5. Thicken the stew with the remainder of the flour, mixed in a little cold water.

JUNGLE STEW

2 lbs. hamburger or 4 C. left-over meat
2 onions
¼ C. fat
1 C. macaroni (uncooked)
3 (15 oz.) cans cooked kidney beans
salt, pepper
2 (1 lb., 3 oz.) cans tomatoes (5 C.)

1. Brown onions and meat in fat in a skillet.
2. Boil macaroni until tender and drain.
3. Combine all ingredients and simmer for 20 minutes.

KETTLE ON CRANE

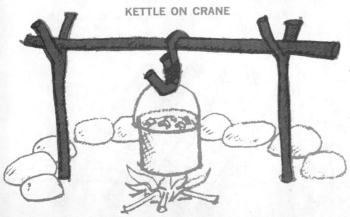

POCKET STEW

Each person brings a vegetable or some bouillon cubes.

4 raw potatoes
1 stalk celery
3 handsful green lima beans
4 raw carrots
1 wedge of cabbage
onions optional
6 or 8 bouillon cubes
seasoning

1. Put 1 C. of water for each person into a kettle and place it on the fire.
2. Bouillon cubes are dropped into the kettle.
3. While waiting for the water to boil, each hiker peels and prepares her own vegetables.
4. When the water is boiling, each cuts up her vegetables into the kettle. When seasoning, remember that bouillon cubes are salty.
5. The stew is done after about ½ hour of boiling.

63

GYPSY STEW

2 onions
5 Tbsp. fat
2 eggs
2 lbs. chopped ham
2 C. cooked rice
flour
salt, pepper
2 (10½ oz.) cans concentrated
vegetable soup, undiluted

1. Dice onions and fry in fat until brown.
2. Mix ham and rice into well-beaten eggs.
3. Form into very small balls.
4. Flour each ball and cook in fat until done.
5. Add salt and pepper to taste while meat and rice balls are cooking.
6. When almost done, pour vegetable soup over them.
7. Cover and heat thoroughly.

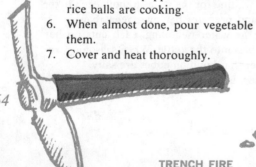

64

TRENCH FIRE

HIKE KOMAC   Northwestern United States

1½ lbs. bacon, diced
3 (10½ oz.) cans concentrated
tomato soup, undiluted
3 onions, diced
3 (15 oz.) cans (5-6 cups) kidney beans
(or other vegetable)
salt, pepper
12 slices toast

1. Use hot quick fire and light frying pan.
2. Fry bacon and onions first. Drain off excess grease and add other ingredients, seasoning to taste.
3. Be sure to drain vegetable so that the stew becomes thick.
4. Serve Hike Komac on hot buttered toast.

SAVORY BEANS

12 link sausages
3 Tbsp. minced onion
3-4 C. cooked corn or 2 (1 lb.) cans
6 C. baked beans or 3 (1 lb.) cans

1. Mince the sausages and fry quickly in a sauce-pan with onion until crisp and brown. If the sausages are very fat, pour off some of the grease.
2. Add cooked corn, cut from the cob, or drained canned corn and baked beans.
3. Stir until well heated; then season as needed, considering the seasoning of the beans.

May be served with cole slaw to which a little catsup has been added.

POET AND PEASANT

⅓ C. butter, fat or oil
8 onions
10 large tart apples, sliced
1½ C. water
1 tsp. salt

1. Heat the fat in a frying pan and slice the onions into it.
2. Cook slowly until nearly tender; then add the apples, water, and salt.
3. Cover and cook until the apples are soft.
4. Remove the cover and fry until the water is all gone, and the onions and apples are a light brown color.

BLUSHING BUNNY

4 Tbsp. butter or margarine
4 Tbsp. flour
1 (3 lb. 3 oz.) can or 5 (10½ oz.) cans
tomato soup (concentrated)
½ lb. cheese, diced
salt, pepper
24 slices toast

1. Melt butter and blend with flour.
2. Add undiluted soup.
3. When thoroughly heated, add cheese. Stir gently until melted.
4. Season and serve on toast.

65

FRIED TOMATOES AND EGGS IN CREAM SAUCE

8 tomatoes
flour
salt, sugar, pepper
vegetable oil
12 slices toast
¼ C. butter or margarine
¼ C. flour
2 C. milk
8 hard-cooked eggs

1. Dip firm slices of unpeeled tomatoes in flour that has been seasoned with salt, sugar, and pepper.
2. Brown the tomatoes quickly in a hot frying pan with a little vegetable oil.
3 Remove the tomatoes and lay the slices on pieces of toast on a hot platter.
4. Melt butter and add the flour.
5. Cook until the mixture begins to bubble, then gradually add the cold milk.
6. Season with 1 tsp. of salt and ¼ tsp. of pepper.

7. Pour this sauce over and around the toast slices, and arrange slices of hot, hard-cooked eggs between and around the tomatoes in the sauce.

RING-TUM-DIDDY

1 lb. bacon, diced
2 large green peppers
3 medium onions
2 (1 lb., 3 oz.) cans tomatoes
3 (1 lb., 3 oz.) cans corn
salt, pepper
½ lb. American cheese, diced
12 slices toast or crackers

1. Dice and fry bacon.
2. Wash, seed, and cut the peppers.
3. Slice the onions thin and add with the peppers to bacon.
4. When onions and peppers are browned, add tomatoes and corn and season to taste.
5. Heat thoroughly and add cheese.
6. Allow cheese to melt and serve on toast or crackers.

66

TOMATO RAREBIT

1 qt. cooked tomatoes or 2 (1 lb.) cans
2 tsp. salt
2 tsp. sugar
¼ tsp. pepper
cayenne pepper
2 Tbsp. chopped onion
1 lb. American cheese, diced
2 Tbsp. butter or margarine
2 eggs
toast or crackers

1. Heat tomatoes and add the salt, sugar, pepper, dash of cayenne, and the chopped onion.
2. When hot, add the diced cheese gradually while stirring constantly.
3. When smooth, add butter and pour over the beaten eggs, stirring all the while.
4. Serve on slices of hot buttered toast or hot crackers.

Makes a good "Friday Dish."

RIBETO

1 lb. rice
grease
2 medium onions
1 (10½ oz.) can concentrated
tomato soup, undiluted
1 (12 oz.) can corned beef
1 (1 lb., 3 oz.) can garden peas
salt, pepper

1. Cook rice until well done.
2. While rice is cooking, cut onions into small pieces and fry in hot grease.
3. When onions are brown, pour in undiluted tomato soup; add shredded corned beef and heat.
4. Heat peas separately.
5. Put a mound of rice in the center of each plate. Fill the rice nest with peas.
6. Pour tomato soup, onions, and meat mixture over this.

Goes well with tossed salad.

67

KIDNEY BEANS AND SPAGHETTI

4 C. dried kidney beans
4 tsp. salt
2 C. spaghetti, uncooked
4 C. stewed tomatoes (2 16 oz. cans)
⅓ C. fat
⅓ C. flour
½ tsp. pepper

1. Wash and soak the beans overnight.
2. Add 2 tsp. of salt, and cook beans until tender (about 1 to 1½ hrs.).
3. Break the spaghetti into pieces about 1 in. long and cook in boiling salted water until soft (about 10 to 15 minutes), then drain.
4. Make a tomato sauce as follows: melt the fat, add the flour, and cook until bubbling. Add the tomatoes and cook until thickened.
5. Mix the spaghetti and beans together.
6. Add seasoning and sauce, and serve hot.

Have something to nibble on while the food is cooking.

68

SAUSAGE AND SPAGHETTI

24 link sausages
3 or 4 (1 lb.) cans of spaghetti
with tomato sauce and cheese

1. Cook the sausages in a hot frying pan, turning them frequently until they are golden brown and tender.
2. Pour off the excess fat; then add the spaghetti mixture and continue cooking until the spaghetti is thoroughly heated.
3. Serve two sausages and a generous amount of spaghetti to each person.

HUNTER FIRE

HOPPING JOHN   Southeastern United States

4 C. cooked black-eyed peas
4 C. cooked rice
1 lb. bacon
2 onions
salt, pepper

1. Cut bacon into small pieces and fry until crisp.
2. Slice onions and fry in the bacon fat.
3. Combine all ingredients in large skillet or saucepan and heat thoroughly.

SQUAW CORN

12 slices bacon
3 large onions
3 (1 lb., 13 oz.) cans corn
salt, pepper
12 slices toast or crackers

1. Cut bacon and onions into small pieces and fry until brown.
2. Add corn and season to taste.
3. Heat well and serve on toast or crackers. Green peppers may be added if desired.

CORN OYSTERS

2 C. cooked or canned corn
4 eggs
1 C. milk
2 Tbsp. melted butter or margarine
½ tsp. salt
1 tsp. baking powder
2 C. flour

This recipe requires a steady fire so that the frying fat will remain at a constant temperature.

1. To the corn add well-beaten eggs, milk, butter, and salt.
2. Beat in the flour and baking powder to make a drop batter.
3. Drop by spoonfuls into hot, deep fat and fry as you would crullers.
4. Drain on absorbent paper and serve with chili sauce or catsup.
5. If the corn oysters are to be served as a main dish, honey, powdered sugar, or sirup may be served with them.

69

CORN YUM-YUM

15 slices bacon
3 onions, diced
4 (1 lb. 13 oz.) cans or 7-8 C. corn
¾ lb. American cheese, diced or grated
8 eggs
salt, pepper
12 slices of toast

1. Cut bacon into small pieces.
2. Fry in a kettle and pour off most of the fat, keeping enough to fry the diced onions.
3. When onions are browned, add corn and heat thoroughly.
4. Add the cheese and stir constantly until melted.
5. Add eggs, one at a time, beating each into the mixture.
6. Cook until slightly thickened (10 minutes).
7. Season well and serve on toast.

Goes well with cole slaw or tossed salad.

BAGS OF GOLD

4 C. flour
2 Tbsp. baking powder
1 tsp. salt
5 Tbsp. shortening
water or milk for desired consistency
(approx. 1⅓-1½ C.)
1 lb. American cheese, cut into ½ in. cubes
4 cans (10½ oz.) tomato soup (concentrated)

1. Make up dough as you would for biscuits. (See Chapter 11 or use 3 C. of prepared biscuit mix.)
2. Roll dough into round balls around a cube of cheese in the center.
3. Drop balls into hot tomato soup (diluted with ½ soup can of water) and cook slowly until dough is cooked through—about 15 to 20 minutes.
4. Keep lid on tightly; do not peek. Serve dumplings with soup as sauce.
5. Add more water to soup before the next batch of dumplings is cooked.

YOKI SPECIAL

1 lb. bacon
2 large onions
2 (1 lb.) cans tomatoes
2 (1 lb.) cans peas
3 (16 oz.) cans spaghetti with cheese sauce
cracker crumbs to thicken
12 slices of bread

1. Fry bacon in small pieces.
2. Remove from the fat and fry the onions.
3. Add tomatoes, peas, spaghetti.
4. If needed, thicken with cracker crumbs.
5. Add bacon. Serve on bread.

SPANISH RICE

3 C. rice
3 qts. water
1½ lb. bacon
4 onions, diced
¼ tsp. pepper
2 (16 oz.) cans tomatoes
½ tsp. sugar
1 tsp. salt

1. Wash rice and cook in 3 qts. of boiling salted water.
2. When done, drain if necessary.
3. Cut bacon and onions into small pieces and fry in a kettle.
4. Combine all ingredients and cook for 15-20 minutes.

KARTOFFEL PFANNKUCHEN   Germany

(Potato Pancakes)

12 medium potatoes
2 tsp. salt
3 onions
3 eggs
1 C. flour (or enough to hold mixture together)

1. Grate half the potatoes, half the onions, then the remainder of potatoes and onions.
2. Add salt, the well-beaten eggs, and flour to thicken the mixture.
3. Cook as pancakes and serve with stewed apples (or applesauce) on top.

(Season the applesauce with lemon juice, nutmeg, or cinnamon, if desired.)

71

BANANA FRITTERS WITH ORANGE SAUCE

3 C. flour
4 tsp. baking powder
½ tsp. salt
2 eggs
1⅓ C. milk
4 bananas

1. Mix flour, baking powder, and salt.
2. Beat eggs, add milk, and stir into the dry ingredients.
3. Remove skins from bananas; cut the fruit into small bits and stir into the batter.
4. Drop by tablespoonfuls into hot fat and fry to a delicate brown.
5. Serve with the following sauce:

Orange Sauce

4 oranges
1 lemon
1 C. sugar
1 C. boiling water

1. Remove the skin from the oranges and slice.
2. Add the juice of one lemon, sugar, and boiling water. Let boil two minutes and serve while hot.

APFEL PFANNKUCHEN Germany
(Apple Pancakes)

6 C. flour
2 tsp. salt
3 Tbsp. baking powder
¼ C. melted shortening
3 eggs, well-beaten
4 C. milk
6 apples

1. Mix dry ingredients.
2. Add to these the well-beaten eggs and shortening.
3. Stir in the milk.
4. After peeling the apples, cut them into thin slices and put them in the batter.
5. Bake as regular pancakes on griddle or in skillet and serve them with sugar sprinkled over the top.

APPLESAUCE PANCAKES

5 C. flour
2 Tbsp. baking powder
1 tsp. cinnamon
1 qt. (3 oz. can) applesauce (unsweetened)
6 Tbsp. sirup or sugar
¼ C. melted shortening
2 eggs

1. Mix the flour with baking powder and cinnamon.
2. Add applesauce, made rather thin, and stir to a batter.
3. Add sirup or sugar, shortening, and well-beaten eggs.
4. Bake on griddle or in skillet.
5. Serve as usual with butter and sirup.

For a more elaborate version, the cakes may be made small and thin, rolled after baking, dusted with powdered sugar, each garnished with a small fried apple ball, and thus dressed up enough to appear at a company breakfast.

BANANA NUT PANCAKES WITH LEMON SAUCE

2 C. pancake mix
2 C. milk
2 bananas, mashed
½ C. nutmeats, cut fine

1. Combine pancake mix with milk and stir until smooth.
2. Add bananas and nuts and blend well.
3. Bake on hot griddle and serve with the following sauce:

Lemon Sauce

1 C. sugar
½ C. water
¼ C. light corn sirup
2 tsp. butter or margarine
3 Tbsp. lemon juice

1. Combine sugar, water, and sirup and boil for 5 minutes.
2. Add the melted butter and lemon juice, stir well, and serve hot.

73

NALASNIKI   Poland
(Pancakes)

4 eggs
½ Tbsp. butter or margarine
1 C. flour
salt
1 Tbsp. sugar
1 pint milk
cheese filling

1. Beat the egg yolks.
2. Add melted butter, salt, sugar, milk, and flour gradually.
3. Add stiffly beaten egg whites.
4. Drop a spoonful of batter into a greased griddle and fry on both sides. (Cakes must be very thin.) Spread with prepared cheese filling and fold like an envelope.
5. Fry again for added crispness on both sides and sprinkle with powdered sugar.

Carry clean eggs to camp site packed in flour or marshmallows, or break the eggs for immediate use into a tightly closed jar.

Cheese Filling for Pancakes

2 C. cottage cheese
1 egg
2 Tbsp. milk
2 Tbsp. sugar
½ C. raisins
salt

Mix well and spread.

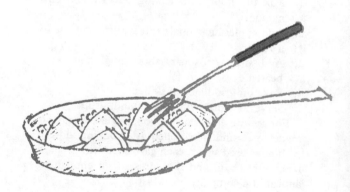

HAWAIIAN ISLANDS
12 slices white bread
¼ lb. butter or margarine
12 slices pineapple
jelly

1. Spread bread with butter and brown on each side in a frying pan.
2. Just before serving put a slice of pineapple and a little juice on each slice, with a spoonful of red jelly in the center of the pineapple.

CRANBERRY APPLESAUCE
3 C. sliced apples
3 C. cranberries
2 C. water
2 C. sugar

1. Combine the apples, cranberries, and water in a saucepan.
2. Cook slowly until soft, then add the sugar—more if the apples are very tart—and cook until the sugar is thoroughly dissolved.

NORWEGIAN PRUNE PUDDING
1 lb. prunes
6 C. boiling water
1 C. sugar
2 tsp. cinnamon
¼ C. cornstarch
2 Tbsp. lemon juice
sweet cream

1. Boil the prunes in 4 C. of boiling water until very tender.
2. Cool them and remove the stones.
3. Add 2 C. water, cinnamon, and sugar and again bring to a boil.
4. Mix cornstarch in a small amount of cold water and add slowly.
5. Cook until thick.
6. Add lemon juice and chill.
7. Serve with cream.

Before washing, rinse dishes used for sugar or flour mixtures in hot water; rinse dishes used for eggs or milk in cold water.

75

CHOCOLATE SAUCE

1 C. sugar
2 Tbsp. cornstarch
3 Tbsp. cocoa
3 Tbsp. butter or margarine
1 C. boiling water
½ C. cold water
½ tsp. vanilla

1. Mix sugar, cocoa, and cornstarch with cold water.
2. Add boiling water and cook over fire until mixture thickens.
3. Add butter and vanilla and beat well.

BUTTERSCOTCH SAUCE

2 C. brown sugar
3 Tbsp. cornstarch
½ C. cold water
1½ C. boiling water
1 tsp. vanilla
¼ C. butter or margarine

1. Mix brown sugar, cornstarch, and cold water.
2. Add boiling water and cook slowly until the mixture thickens.
3. Add butter; remove from fire and add vanilla.
4. Beat well.

SHORT-CUT FUDGE

6 (1 oz.) sq. unsweetened chocolate
2⅔ C. (2 cans) condensed (sweetened) milk
2 tsp. butter or margarine
2 Tbsp. vanilla
4 C. confectioner's sugar
1 C. chopped dates (1 lb.)
1 C. chopped nuts

1. Melt chocolate over low heat.
2. Add condensed milk and cook 5 minutes, stirring occasionally until mixture thickens.
3. Remove from fire, add butter and vanilla, and work in confectioner's sugar.
4. Fold in dates and nuts.
5. Pour into a shallow, buttered pan.
6. Chill and cut in squares.

COCOA FUDGE

⅔ C. cocoa
4 C. sugar
2 Tbsp. light corn sirup
¼ C. butter or margarine
1 C. milk
dash of salt
1 tsp. vanilla

1. Mix cocoa and sugar in a saucepan.
2. Add sirup, butter, and milk and mix thoroughly.
3. Cook over low heat, stirring until sugar is melted.
4. Remove from heat when a sample of the mixture forms a medium hard ball in cold water.
5. Cool without stirring; add salt and vanilla and beat until creamy.
6. Pour into a buttered platter and cut into squares when hard.
7. Chopped nuts and raisins or flaked coconut may be added, if desired.

CANDIED APPLES

4 C. sugar
¼ lb. butter or margarine
2 C. corn sirup
12 apples

1. Mix sugar, butter, and sirup in a kettle and cook, stirring constantly until mixture spins a thread when tested.
2. Place apples on sticks, dip into the sirup, and twirl in the air until cool.

COCONUT CREAM CANDY
Southeastern United States

1 coconut (fresh meat and milk)
3 C. sugar

1. Combine sugar with coconut milk and boil for 10 minutes.
2. Then add grated coconut and cook 5 minutes.
3. Remove from fire and beat until mixture is cold.
4. Pour out on a greased surface and cut in squares.

77

CORN FLAKE CHEWS

2 C. brown sugar
½ C. maple sirup
2 Tbsp. butter or margarine
6 C. corn flakes

1. Cook sugar and sirup over moderate heat, stirring constantly until sugar dissolves and mixture bubbles for about 7 minutes or until sirup spins a thread when tested.
2. Add butter.
3. Pour mixture over corn flakes that have been placed in a buttered mixing bowl.
4. Stir so that each corn flake is coated.
5. Drop by teaspoonfuls onto waxed paper or a buttered surface.

POPCORN BALLS

2 qts. popcorn
1 C. molasses
1 C. brown sugar
1 Tbsp. butter or margarine
½ C. water
pinch of salt

1. Boil molasses, sugar, butter, salt, and water until it forms a hard ball in cold water.
2. Pour over freshly popped corn.
3. Mix well, form into balls, and let harden.

CHOCOLATE POPCORN

3 qts. popcorn
1½ C. sugar
1½ Tbsp. butter or margarine
1 (1 oz.) sq. unsweetened chocolate
¼ C. water

1. Cook all the ingredients together until mixture spins a long thread when tested.
2. While sirup is hot, pour it over 3 qts. of freshly popped and picked-over corn.
3. Stir until all the kernels are coated.

PAN POPPED CORN

3 qt. pan with lid
¼ C. salad oil
½ C. popcorn
¼ C. melted butter or margarine
salt

1. Heat heavy pan.
2. Add oil and heat until 2-3 corn kernels spin in the oil.
3. Then add all popcorn and cover securely. Hold lid on if necessary.
4. Shake gently until you hear last of popping.

SNOW ON THE MOUNTAIN

6 milk chocolate bars (1½ oz. size)
1 C. coconut (shredded or flaked)
36 soda crackers

1. Melt chocolate bars (or sweetened chocolate) in a greased pan.
2. Dip a spoonful onto each soda cracker and sprinkle with coconut.

SNOWBALLS

1⅓ C. sugar
1 Tbsp. melted fat
3 eggs, well-beaten
1 C. sour milk
¼ tsp. nutmeg
1 tsp. salt
½ tsp. soda
4 tsp. baking powder
3 C. flour
powdered sugar

1. Add sugar, melted fat, sour milk, and beaten eggs to mixed dry ingredients.
2. Then add enough flour to handle.
3. Roll out ¼ in. thick and cut with small round cutter about 1 in. in diameter.
4. Fry in deep fat, turning the balls as soon as they come to the top.
5. When cool, roll in powdered sugar.

To sour milk, add 1 Tbsp. of vinegar or lemon juice to 1 C. milk and let stand 5 minutes.

79

SUGARING OFF   Northeastern United States

maple sap or sirup

snow

1. Boil down sap or sirup until drops of the liquid form a hard ball when poured into 1 C. of cold water.
2. Then pour the maple sirup on clean snow and let it harden into sugar cakes that can be eaten as candy.

Variation

In the South, cane sirup may be used instead of maple sap or sirup. Cook to hard ball stage. Cool and pull like taffy.

MOLASSES TAFFY
(pulled)

3 C. molasses

1½ C. brown sugar

1½ Tbsp. vinegar

1½ Tbsp. butter or margarine

⅓ tsp. soda

1. Boil ingredients together until brittle when dropped into cold water.
2. Pour into greased pans.
3. When cooled enough to handle it, wet hands in cold water (warm hands make candy stick) or grease them with shortening or butter.
4. Stretch a lump of candy and double it up.
5. Continue until light colored.
6. Cut into small pieces.

PRALINES   Southeastern United States

4 C. brown sugar

⅔ C. butter or margarine

½ C. sweet milk

4 C. chopped pecans

1. Stir milk, sugar, and butter together over a slow fire until sugar is dissolved.
2. Add nuts and boil until mixture forms a hard ball in cold water.
3. Beat until mixture cools.
4. Drop by spoonfuls on waxed paper. Allow sufficient room between pralines.

HONEY RAISIN BRITTLE

3 C. puffed rice
3 C. seedless raisins
1 C. sugar
½ C. water
¼ tsp. salt
2 Tbsp. butter or margarine
½ C. honey

1. Heat the puffed rice in the oven until kernels will crush between the fingers.
2. Warm the raisins in the oven. Also warm a mixing bowl and a buttered pan.
3. Boil the sugar, honey, and water until a sample of the mixture forms a hard ball when tested in cold water.
4. Add salt and butter.
5. When the mixture comes to a boil again, remove from the fire and pour over raisins and puffed rice in the warm bowl.
6. Mix thoroughly and pour into a buttered pan.
7. Allow to harden, loosen at edges and turn out of the pan. Cut into strips.

DATE LOAF CANDY

3 C. sugar
1 C. milk
1¼ C. chopped dates (8 oz.)
1 C. pecans

1. Cook sugar and milk until a hard ball forms when a sample of the mixture is dropped into cold water.
2. Add pecans and chopped dates; stir well and remove from fire.
3. Beat until dates become pulpy.
4. Pour mixture onto a wet cloth; roll and let stand until cool. Slice and serve.

SPICED MILK

2 tsp. cinnamon
½ tsp. nutmeg
3½ qts. milk

1. Mix spices and scald milk. Do not boil.
2. Add spices to milk and stir thoroughly. Sugar may be added if desired.

COCOA

⅔ C. cocoa
1½ C. water
¼ tsp. salt
⅔ C. sugar
3 qts. milk
1 tsp. vanilla

1. Mix cocoa, water, salt, and sugar.
2. Bring to a boiling point; then simmer 5 minutes.
3. Add scalded milk and vanilla.
4. Serve hot, topped with marshmallows.

Cocoa may be chilled and served cold. Use fresh, evaporated or reconstituted milk.

HOT CHOCOLATE

4 (1 oz.) sq. chocolate
½ tsp. salt
1 C. sugar
3 qts. milk
1 tsp. vanilla

1. Melt chocolate; add salt, sugar, and 1 pt. of milk.
2. Cook until mixture begins to thicken.
3. Then add 2½ qts. of scalded milk and vanilla.
4. Serve hot with marshmallows.

This may be made in advance, chilled, and served cold. Fresh, evaporated, or reconstituted dry milk may be used.

10. TOASTING, BROILING, PLANKING

To the uninitiated, the words outdoor cooking probably calls to mind visions of steaks sizzling, marshmallows toasting, beef barbecuing, corn roasting, and hot dogs hissing over glowing coals. The real outdoor cook knows that these foods are the rewards of long experience, beginning with simple skillet or kettle meals for which even a flaming fire is sufficient. She is therefore in a much better position to produce a delectable dish.

Glowing coals are the right fire for toasting, broiling, and planking. A flame burns the surface of the foods on a toasting fork, while its smoke coats the meat or marshmallow with soot. For the cook who can't wait for the flames and smoke to spend themselves, thus making the necessary coals, the skillet is better than the toaster. It is the younger, inexperienced cook who covers her impatience by saying "but I like my marshmallows burned." It must be admitted that there is a fascination to seeing how many burned coats can be removed from a single marshmallow, but it's more of an engineering feat than a cooking skill.

To cook food directly over the heat, whether it is a main dish meat or a dessert delicacy, you must use some sort of device for holding the food. You can put a slice of steak directly on the coals but that is close to ember cooking which you can read up on in Chapter 13. That chapter also has more details on using charcoal.

The wood fire that produces good coals needs hardwoods and can be laid as a Basic A, tepee, or log cabin fire on the ground in a cleared area, in a trench, or in an improvised fireplace or backyard barbecue (see Chapter 4). Because it takes longer to get coals than to get a flame, start fire 30 minutes or so before you need the heat for cooking. This is the kind of planning the experienced cooks can see the reason for, but it is frequently forgotten or ignored by the hungry novice who then eats

smoky food burned in the flame. When and if more fuel is needed, add it to the side of a bed of coals and rake the coals it eventually makes over the big bed of coals. This keeps flames and smoke away from the food.

Utensils need long enough handles to protect the cook from the heat of the coals. It is

84

possible to lash a stick or length of doweling to a fork, spoon, toasting grill, or toasting fork. Wet wooden dowel sticks or dead sticks covered with aluminum foil are most effective for working over hot coals. When you are finished using a stick, save it for future cookouts.

In choosing food to broil directly over the heat: (1) choose meat with a little fat and start it over the heat so that the fat is on the top side (usually with the skin side up on chicken, for example), so the meat is self-basting; (2) baste very lean meats with an oil, fat, or flavored marinade such as French or Italian salad dressing by brushing it on with a pastry brush, a swab of cloth lashed to the end of the stick, or spooned with a long handle.

Direct heat adds a flavor bonus to all foods but because it is a quick cooking method you have to choose tender foods (young chicken) or have less tender ones cut in small pieces (such as ground beef or hamburgers or small

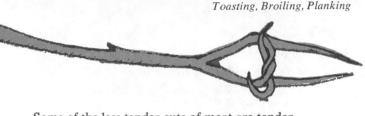

pieces of round steak for kabobs).

When food is cooked by direct heat, it is best when eaten as soon as it is ready. Therefore, be sure you have everything else ready when you start the cooking—or be sure that other things will be timed to be eaten at just the right moment.

The recipes that follow call for a variety of foods—meats, vegetables, breads, and fruits.

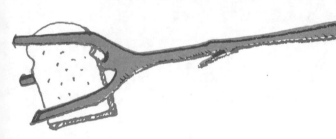

They include recipes that are easy on the budget and more expensive treats—take your pick.

Some of the less tender cuts of meat are tenderized by the ingredients of the barbecue sauce used. Originally, barbecue meant a pork or beef carcass cooked whole over the coals. Now it more or less means pieces of meat that are basted while cooked over direct heat. You use your own special sauce or choose one from these recipes. Among these recipes are also some for main courses, desserts, breakfasts, lunches, or dinners.

The new cook should look for simplicity, quick preparation, simple equipment, single or at most only a few ingredients, and short cooking time. Toasting sandwiches brought from home or spread at the fireside is a tasty beginning. Cheese, peanut butter, ham, or luncheon meats are good fillings for toasted sandwiches. Toasting the bread on the spot for a vegetable or fruit sandwich is even easier for the young beginner. Some special spreads are included in the following recipe list. With experience comes the patience for elaborate items.

BREAD TWISTERS OR DOUGHBOYS
(see Chapter 11)

6 C. flour
¼ C. baking powder
1 tsp. salt
2 or 3 C. water (to desired consistency)
¼ C. shortening

or 6 cups of biscuit mix and water

1. Mix dough, pinch off small portion, and mold into a long patty.
2. Wrap it around the end of a stick in a spiral twist.
3. Knead cracks together and bake over hot coals (about 20 min.).

Variations

Bacon Twisters: Cook bacon, which is twisted around end of stick. Cover with dough and bake. Eat as bacon sandwich.

Hamburger Twisters: Cook hamburger on end of stick until it is golden brown. Cover with dough and bake. Eat as sandwich.

Jam or Jelly Twisters: Cook a bread twister, slip it off the stick, and fill the hole with butter and jam or jelly. Be sure that the dough covers the end of the stick so there will be a closed end to the twister.

Cheese and Raisin Twisters: Cook a bread twister, slip it off the stick, and fill the hole with raisins and diced American cheese or cottage cheese.

ANGELS ON HORSEBACK

24 slices bacon
24 1-in. sq. of American cheese
24 buns or rolls

1. Wrap a square of cheese in a thin slice of bacon.
2. Pierce with a stick so it holds bacon securely and broil over the coals, turning in order to keep cheese from dripping into fire.
3. Have roll ready to make sandwich as soon as bacon is ready.

87

MEAL-ON-A-SKEWER

2 lbs. ground beef
1 egg, beaten
½ C. bread crumbs
½ tsp. salt
¼ tsp. pepper
tomato wedges
12 frankfurter rolls

1. Mix beef, egg, and crumbs.
2. Season.
3. Using 1 Tbsp. of mixture for each ball, form into 36 small balls.
4. Take skewers and thread meat balls onto some, tomato wedges onto others.
5. Cook about 3 in. from heat, turning to brown evenly.
6. Combine meat and tomatoes in heated rolls.

BACON-BANANA-ON-A-STICK

6 bananas
12 strips bacon
12 frankfurter rolls

1. Cut peeled, green-tipped or all-yellow bananas in half, crosswise.
2. Put green stick, toasting skewer, or toasting fork through one end of a bacon strip and then lengthwise through a banana half.
3. Wrap the strip of bacon in a spiral around the banana.
4. Fasten free end on the stick, skewer, or fork.
5. Toast over hot coals until bacon is crisp, about 5 minutes.
6. Slide from stick or fork into a roll which may be toasted beforehand, if desired.

HIKER'S KNAPSACK

24 thin slices of ham
24 thin slices of processed cheese
12 slices pineapple
24 buns

1. Fold a slice of ham over a slice of cheese and half a slice of pineapple.
2. Fasten the edges with small twigs.
3. Broil knapsacks over hot coals until both sides of the ham are a golden brown and the cheese is melted.
4. Serve on a hot buttered bun.

PIGS IN BLANKETS

4 C. flour
2 Tbsp. baking powder
1½ tsp. salt
3 Tbsp. sugar
6 Tbsp. shortening
water or milk for desired consistency
24 link pork sausages (or canned Vienna sausages)

1. Mix dough as for biscuits.
2. Pinch off small pieces of dough and flatten into strips or elongated patties.
3. Wrap each sausage link (which has been seared in a hot skillet) in a strip of dough.
4. Knead the sides of the dough together so that the sausage is completely covered.
5. Cook in a reflector oven or on a pointed stick.
6. Pigs in blankets may also be cooked indoors in a hot oven.

Be sure sausage is completely cooked.

PIONEER DRUMSTICKS

3 lbs. chopped beef
1 C. cornflakes, crumbled fine
2 eggs (optional)
12 rolls or 24 slices of bread
salt, pepper, onion (if desired)

1. Mix beef, seasonings, eggs, and cornflakes together thoroughly.
2. Wrap a portion around the end of a stick, squeezing in place evenly. Make it long and thin, not a ball. Be sure there are no air spaces in it. (Watch out for big pieces of cornflakes.)
3. Cook slowly over coals, turning frequently so all sides are evenly cooked.
4. Twist slightly to take off stick.
5. Serve in a roll.

Some prefer to roll the meat in crumbled cornflakes after placing it on the stick to make a crust. Try it both ways.

89

KABOBS

3 lbs. round steak cut in small pieces, trimmed of
fat, about 1 in. by ¼ in. thick
8 small onions, peeled and sliced
8 partially boiled tomatoes; if desired,
sliced ¼ in. thick
24 strips bacon, cut in squares
24 rolls or bread for sandwiches

1. Place pieces of steak, onion, bacon, and tomato alternately on sticks, pushing them
   down the stick and leaving a little space between pieces. Ingredients may be divided and
   half cooked at one time so that everyone has
   "seconds."
2. Repeat in same order.
3. Sear quickly all over by holding close to
   coals.
4. Then cook slowly a little away from coals,
   turning until done.

Frankfurter Kabobs

Alternate pieces of frankfurter, canned white
potatoes, small whole onions.

Ham Kabobs

Alternate ham cubes, canned sweet potatoes,
and pineapple chunks.

Liver Kabobs

Use small pieces of liver (beef, lamb, or calf)
and pieces of bacon.

Oyster Kabobs

Use oysters and pieces of bacon.

Shish Kabobs   Near Eastern
(roasted meat on skewers)

1. Alternate 1 in. cubes of young lamb with tomato, bay leaf, and onion.
2. Broil over coals.

Teriyaki   Japanese

3 (20 oz.) cans pineapple chunks (drained)
3 lbs. top round or sirloin of beef in ¾ in. cubes
monosodium glutamate
24 olives (stuffed)

1. Drain pineapple and save sirup for sauce (see
   page 95).
2. Cut beef into cubes like pineapple chunks.

90

3. Marinate beef in Teriyaki sauce for at least 1 hour.
4. Alternate meat and pineapple on 24 skewers, ending with olives.
5. Sprinkle with monosodium glutamate.
6. Broil.

FRANKFURTERS

1. Cook over fire in grill or on toasting stick.
2. Serve in buns with a tomato sauce.

HEAVENLY HOT DOGS

1 dozen hot dogs
12 slices bacon
½ lb. American cheese

1. Slit hot dogs lengthwise (but not all the way through)
2. Put strip of cheese in slit.
3. Wrap bacon around to hold all together.
4. Put on toasting stick or fork.

HOT DOGS SUPREME

24 frankfurters
1 (8 oz.) jar sweet pickle relish
24 slices bacon
prepared mustard, catsup, or onions
24 long rolls

1. Split frankfurters on one side and fill with relish.
2. Wrap with a slice of bacon and fasten the ends of the bacon around the frankfurter with the aid of small twigs. (Arrange bacon around the frankfurter to hold the relish.)
3. Pierce the frankfurter with a stick and broil over hot coals until the bacon is crisp and the frankfurter is cooked.
4. Serve on hot rolls with mustard, catsup, or onions.

91

PLANKED FISH

4 lbs. fish
bacon strips
3 Tbsp. shortening
butter or margarine
salt, pepper
lemon juice

1. Select a slab of sweet hardwood (birch, maple, apple) 2 or 3 in. thick, 2 ft. long and somewhat wider than the opened fish.
2. Prop it in front of a bed of coals until it is sizzling hot or place in the fire to char.
3. Split the fish down the back but do not cut through the belly skin.
4. Clean and wipe it quite dry.
5. Grease the plank and spread the fish out on it like an open book, the skin side down. A few pieces of bacon may be spread over the fish for basting.
6. Secure the fish to the plank with pegs whittled from hardwood or with wire nails.
7. Prop before a reflector fire.
8. When the fish becomes flaky it is done.

9. Sprinkle with salt, pepper, lemon juice, and butter and serve while hot.

PLANKED STEAK

3 or 4 lbs. of steak
butter or margarine
salt, pepper
shortening

1. Prepare slab of sweet hardwood as directed for the planked fish.
2. Season steak, grease the plank, and place a few bits of shortening on the steak, which is anchored to the plank with wooden pegs or wire nails.
3. Prop before a reflector fire, broil on both sides, and serve while hot.

SALMON STEAK

12 salmon steaks
butter or margarine

1. Broil steaks over coals.
2. Baste with butter during cooking.

HAM

3 slices tenderized ham (1 in. thick)
pineapple basting sauce

1. Marinate ham in sauce for at least 30 minutes.
2. Broil 6 minutes.
3. Baste with sauce.
4. Turn and broil other side 6 minutes.

BARBECUED CHICKEN, METHOD 1

unsplit roasting chickens
(½ lb. per camper)

Chickens should be cleaned, dressed, singed over flames, then washed with warm water and baking soda, inside and out. By the time the chickens are ready, the fire and fireplace should also be ready.

Build a reflector fireplace with two uprights and a spit for the chickens. The uprights should be 2 or 3 feet high and placed about 1 foot in front of the reflector. The fire is then built between the uprights and the reflector and allowed to burn for about 1 hour or until there is an ample bed of glowing embers. (See illustration on chapter tab.)

Run the spit through the middle of the chickens, all in the same position, tie securely with wet stout cord, and place on the uprights over the coals. The chickens should cook slowly at first. If the uprights have notches or crotches at 2 or 3 intervals, the spit may then be lowered or raised, according to the heat of the fire and the condition of the chicken. Turn spit occasionally so all sides of the chicken cook. It may be necessary to add wood to the fire, but keep flames as low as possible.

Cook slowly for at least 2½ or 3 hours. The length of time depends upon the size of the chickens and on the fire. When the meat is dry inside, it is done. If pink and juicy when cut with a knife, return to fire for further cooking.

It is important to use hardwoods, such as oak, maple, locust, hickory, beech, birch, walnut, pecan, hornbeam, ironwood, eucalyptus, mesquite, or apple in order to produce lasting coals.

93

BARBECUED CHICKEN, METHOD 2

Use broilers in place of roasters. Split the chickens down the center so they will open out flat. Clean as in Method No. 1. Well in advance, dig a trench about 1 foot deep and long enough to take care of the number of chickens to be cooked. Build a fire in the trench, using hardwood, and allow to burn for about 1 hour. When this has burned to coals, place a broiler over the trench. This may be improvised from chicken wire or a similar material. Place the chickens on the wire, opened out, and allow to cook slowly. If they begin to brown immediately, the fire is too hot and some of the coals should be removed. Baste with barbecue sauce.

This method usually requires less time than Method No. 1, but is not as picturesque. One or 1½ hours should be allowed.

BARBECUED PORK

Pork is barbecued in the same manner as chicken. Allow about ¼ lb. to each person. Be quite sure the meat is thoroughly cooked before serving it.

BARBECUED CHOPS OR BEEF

12 lamb chops, 12 small steaks
or 12 pork chops (all about 1 in. thick)

1. Cook any of the above on a grill or spit.
2. Turn often, painting with barbecue sauce.
3. The meat should be cooked very slowly and should brown gradually.

BARBECUED TURKEY OR DUCK

See *Barbecued Chicken,* but allow more time for cooking. Less sauce is needed, especially for duck whose fat makes it self-basting.

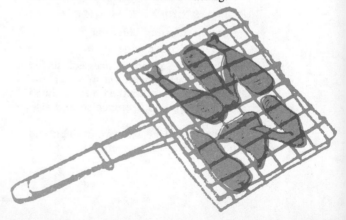

94

BARBECUE SAUCES

For 2 Chickens		For 10 Chickens
½ C.	cooking oil	1½ C.
2½ Tbsp.	salt	⅔ C.
1 C.	cider vinegar	1 qt.
1½ tsp.	poultry seasoning	2 Tbsp.
¼ tsp.	pepper	1 tsp.

1. Mix ingredients in a saucepan.
2. Bring to boil.
3. Keep hot while using to baste chickens.

Teriyaki Sauce   Oriental

1½ C. pineapple sirup (from
20 oz. can of chunks)
¾ C. soy sauce
2 cloves garlic, minced
2 Tbsp. ginger

1. Combine ingredients.
2. Use to marinate meat and for basting.

Pineapple Basting Sauce

1 C. brown sugar
1½ C. cider vinegar
3-6 cloves
6 Tbsp. prepared mustard
3 C. pineapple juice

Simmer together 5 minutes.

CORN ON THE COB

24 ears of corn in husks
salt, pepper
¾ lb. butter or margarine

1. Soak corn (husks and all) in water for a couple of hours.
2. Remove from water and lay ears on grate above bed of coals.
3. Cover with wet burlap or canvas if desired.
4. Turn ears occasionally until done (kernels are no longer juicy or milky when punctured). Takes about ½ hour.
5. Pull back husks to use as handle. Remove silk.
6. Butter and add salt and pepper.

95

TOASTS

Bread is toasted over hot coals to a golden brown and buttered while hot. Raisin, white, or whole wheat toast may be used in the following variations as a bread or as a dessert for meals cooked along the trail. Here are some variations:

Applesauce Toast: Spread a generous layer of applesauce over hot buttered toast.

Cinnamon Toast: Mix cinnamon and sugar and sprinkle over buttered toast for breakfast or a woodland tea.

Chocolate Toast: Use cocoa mixed with sugar instead of cinnamon.

Orange Toast: Moisten sugar with orange juice and mix with grated orange rind. Spread on toast and use for a special breakfast cookout.

Pineapple Toast: Spread crushed pineapple over buttered toast and serve as a dessert. This is extra special with raisin bread.

Apricot Marshmallow Toast: Soak ½ lb. dried apricots overnight and stew in the same water until tender. Drain, press through a sieve, add 4

Tbsp. of sugar and heat. Spread on buttered toast, place a marshmallow in the center of each piece, and tilt before an open fire until the marshmallows are brown. (The apricot mixture can be cooked in advance and placed in a jar until ready to use.)

Bacon and Cheese Toast (Cheese Dreams): Slice or grate cheese on slices of toast, lay a piece of bacon on each piece, and broil before an open fire.

MINTED MARSHMALLOWS

24 marshmallows
chocolate peppermint wafers

1. Carefully toast marshmallows until golden brown.
2. Slide off the fork or stick and slip a chocolate peppermint wafer into each marshmallow.
3. Wait a few seconds for the wafer to melt and the top of the marshmallow to form a slight crust on the outside so that you can pick it up.

MARSHMALLOW APPLE

12 apples
12 marshmallows

1. Core apples.
2. Toast marshmallows. Put marshmallows in the apple holes.

TOASTED TAFFY APPLES

1 apple per person
brown sugar
toasting stick

1. Stick stem end of apple on toasting stick.
2. Roast until skin is ready to peel off.
3. Peel apple and roll in pan of brown sugar.
4. Turning slowly, hold sugared apple over coals to caramelize.

FAIRY RINGS

1 dozen glazed doughnuts
1 dozen marshmallows

1. Put doughnut on stick; then the marshmallow on the end.
2. Toast over fire.

MOCK ANGEL FOOD CAKE

1 loaf day-old unsliced white bread
3 cups coconut (shredded or flaked)
3 tall (14 oz.) cans condensed milk

1. Trim crusts off unsliced bread and slice ¾ in. thick.
2. Then cut into strips ¾ in. thick.
3. Dip in condensed milk until each piece is well covered and then roll each in coconut.
4. Toast over an open fire on a toaster. (Can also be baked in a reflector oven.) When done it will taste like angel food cake. Save bread crusts for cooking purposes.

For variation, the pieces may be rolled in cocoa and sugar, or cinnamon and sugar, instead of coconut.

DOUGHNUT DELIGHTS

24 fresh doughnuts
cream cheese, jelly, or marmalade

1. Cut doughnuts in half and spread each half with cream cheese, jelly, or marmalade.
2. Toast over coals until well heated.

97

SOME-MORES

8 (1½ oz.) milk chocolate bars, the flat kind
without nuts (broken in thirds)
48 graham crackers (about 1 large and 1 or 2
small pkgs.)
24 marshmallows (about ½ lb.)

1. Make a sandwich of a piece of chocolate and
   2 crackers.
2. Toast a marshmallow to a golden brown.
3. Put into sandwiches between chocolate and
   cracker.
4. Press gently together and eat.

Variations

Use peanut butter or toasted peanuts instead
of chocolate. These are sometimes called "Robin-
son Crusoes."

Use slices of apples instead of crackers —
"Apple Some-Mores."

Use chocolate covered crackers and no chocolate bars.

Use chocolate peppermints instead of chocolate bars.

Tastes like "some more."

11. BETTER FOR THE BAKING

There are two varieties of baking outdoors —in a reflector oven (or baker) in front of a fire and in a Dutch oven or foil packet in the fire (coals or ashes). There is more on the use of the Dutch oven and on baking in aluminum foil in Chapter 13.

THE REFLECTOR OVEN

The reflector oven (see illustration on Chapter tab) is not a modern outdoor device. Many a colonial cook or pioneer woman on a trail West had her version of this versatile piece of equipment. They also used the Dutch oven. You may see examples of both in local historical museums.

You can buy or make reflector ovens. Select one that is sturdy and stable. It can be collapsible for convenience in storing and carrying and should be light in weight. Rigid ones take more space for storage and are awkward to carry. These ovens are best suited to camp sites with plenty of storage space for permanent use. Since the food bakes in these ovens by reflected heat rather than by conduction or convection (as it does in a home range oven) it is not necessary to have closed ends, although a foil to the windy side would be useful as a windbreak to ward off cooling drafts.

It is important to have ovens that fit the pans you have. Otherwise, get pans to fit the oven you like—pans that are not wider than the

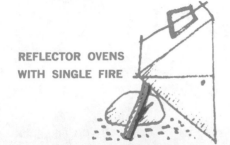

REFLECTOR OVENS WITH SINGLE FIRE

DIRECTIONS FOR MAKING A COOKIE PAN REFLECTOR OVEN

Materials Needed: 5 cookie sheets or pans with turned up edges; 8 bolts with wing nuts; 1 wooden handle with screws.

1. Place 2 sheets (the side sheets) together and bore 4 holes (1 to 4 as indicated on diagram).
2. Bore 1 hole in the lip edge at each end of the third sheet (shelf sheet) at #1 to correspond with holes on the side sheets.
3. Bore 2 holes in the lip edge at each end of the fourth sheet (bottom sheet) at #2 and #3 to correspond with the holes on the side sheets.
4. Bore 1 hole in the lip edge at each end of the top sheet at #4 and screw wooden handle on the outside at #5. This permits cook to open stove from the rear to test baking. The top sheet will swing up when the oven is assembled, since it is bolted only at #4.
5. Assemble oven. Be sure the wing nuts are on the outside. The top sheet should overlap the bottom sheet slightly. If it does not, cover the gap with foil when baking.

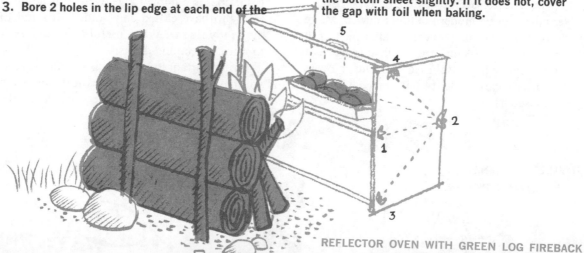

100

REFLECTOR OVEN WITH GREEN LOG FIREBACK

ends of the oven. Two ovens, located to get the best use of the fire, are better than one large two-pan one that is larger than the fire. Raise the oven to the level of the fireplace on sandfilled coffee cans, if necessary.

The oven should be angled so as to reflect the proper heat. The source of heat must be as high and as wide as the oven. It helps to have a reflector behind the cooking fire (see diagrams of reflector fires with rock, clay banks, stacked green logs, metal sheets, and aluminum foil backings—even one made of the fire itself for two-sided use).

Both glowing coals and bright flames produce heat for the oven. This heat is reflected to the top of the food and browns it. Dark surfaces absorb and hold heat, so as the cake browns it takes on even more heat to speed the cooking process. The shiny interior of the oven also reflects every bit of heat possible. The bottom of the cake pan that sits on the rack should be black (as it is in commercial reflector oven sets) to absorb heat for cooking the bottom of the cake, otherwise the browning top cooks faster. If you scrubbed off that black coating, in a burst of housewifely zeal, paint it again with stove blacking or black enamel. Do this for pans you use in your own handmade oven too. If you are already outdoors and have to substitute pans, rub some charcoal from your fire on the bottoms for temporary help.

The fire should provide steady heat, so feed it as needed a little at a time. The oven is usually placed about 10 in. in front of the fire. If you can hold your hand in front of the oven between it and the fire and count slowly to 8 before your hand gets too hot, the oven and fire are just right. To decrease heat in the oven move the baker away from the fire; or move it closer for more heat if you can't increase the fire. Keep other pots and kettles from obstructing the path of the heat from fire to oven.

You can bake anything in this baker that you could in your gas or electric oven at home. Even small angel food cakes have been successfully baked However, they are not for the beginning cook or the novice fire builder because they need careful handling and carefully controlled slow, steady heat. Flavorful cookies and cakes such as gingerbread, spice, chocolate, and molasses recipes are good choices. They are tasty enough without any special topping. White or yellow cakes usually need an icing or at least a topping—one more process to take your time and delay your eating when you are already hungry for the treat. Biscuits—as toppings for fruit cobblers and as a base for quick coffee cakes—are happy choices too. Mixes for these as well as for muffins and cornbreads are very useful because they require few utensils on the site and few additional ingredients. Choose those that need the fewest additions if packing, carrying, and lack of outdoor storage space and refrigeration are considerations. Commercial mixes with clear directions work well and so do your own homemade mixes.

Casseroles made at home can be baked reflectively but are easier to do in a Dutch oven or imu (see Chapters 11 and 13). Individual meat loaves cook quickly and well. Be sure that the onions in them are chopped very fine and that the loaves are well done, especially if they contain pork.

Many favorite home oven recipes can be used outdoors. Here are a few regular recipes, some special outdoor recipes, and some from other countries and different regions of the U.S.A.

See page 156 for instructions on how to make a cardboard box oven.

EGGS IN TOMATO CUPS

12 medium-sized tomatoes
salt
1½ C. grated American cheese
12 eggs
1¼ C. evaporated milk
paprika
12 slices toast

1. Scoop out the tomatoes, leaving a thick shell.
2. Dredge each with salt and put in a pan with a little water.
3. In the bottom of each tomato put 1 Tbsp. of grated American cheese.
4. Bake 10 minutes in a reflector oven.
5. Then drop a raw egg in each, put back in the oven, and cook about 15 minutes or until the eggs are set.
6. Serve each tomato on a slice of toast with the following sauce: stir together over the fire 10 Tbsp. of grated cheese and the evaporated milk until the cheese is melted and the mixture is smooth. Add salt and paprika to taste.

MACARONI AND CHEESE

¾ lb. macaroni
2 tsp. salt
1 qt. milk
1 lb. American cheese, cubed
2 C. bread crumbs
⅓ C. butter or margarine
paprika

1. Boil the macaroni in a large amount of water to which 2 tsp. of salt have been added.
2. When tender, drain and rinse.
3. Scald milk, add cheese cubes and continue stirring the hot milk over a low flame until the cheese is melted.
4. Combine the macaroni and cheese sauce.
5. Pour into a baking dish and cover with bread crumbs and butter.
6. Sprinkle with paprika and bake in a reflector oven until the bread crumbs are brown — about ½ hour.

103

SWEET POTATOES AND APPLES

4 lbs. sweet potatoes, peeled and parboiled
2 to 3 lbs. apples
1 C. sugar
salt
2 to 8 Tbsp. butter or margarine
1 tsp. cinnamon
1 C. milk or water

1. Cut partially cooked (parboiled) potatoes and apples into uniform pieces.
2. Arrange in alternate layers with mixture of cinnamon, sugar, and salt, and dots of butter between.
3. Add milk or water.
4. Bake in a reflector oven ½ hour, or until potatoes and apples are done.

SWEET POTATO AND ORANGE CASSEROLE

5 lbs. sweet potatoes
juice of 5 oranges
1 C. raisins
salt
½ C. brown sugar
⅛ lb. butter

1. Boil potatoes.
2. Then peel, mash, and mix thoroughly with orange juice and raisins.
3. Salt to taste.
4. Put a layer of potatoes in the bottom of a well-greased baking dish.
5. Sprinkle with brown sugar and dots of butter.
6. Put in the rest of the potatoes and again sprinkle with sugar and butter.
7. Bake in a reflector oven from ½ to 1 hour.

VOLCANO POTATOES

12 potatoes (white or sweet)
½ C. butter
pepper
2¼ tsp. salt
paprika
1 C. milk
3 Tbsp. grated cheese

1. Pare, cook, and mash potatoes until smooth and light.
2. Add butter, a few grains of pepper, salt, and paprika to taste, with sufficient milk to moisten thoroughly.
3. Make into irregular cones about 3 in. high and place on a platter for baking.
4. In the top of each cone make a deep indentation. Mix the grated cheese with a little salt and enough paprika to make it quite red, and fill each cone with this mixture.
5. Sprinkle more cheese over the cones and place in a hot oven. As the cheese melts it will spread and cover the sides of the cones.

SCALLOPED CHIPPED BEEF AND POTATOES

½ C. butter or margarine
½ C. flour
½ tsp. salt
5 C. milk
¼ C. chopped onions
16 potatoes
¾ lb. chipped beef

1. Melt 6 Tbsp. of the butter.
2. Add flour and salt and cook until bubbling.
3. Add milk gradually, stirring constantly, and cook until smooth and thick.
4. Fry onions quickly in 2 Tbsp. of butter.
5. Place a layer of thinly sliced potatoes in a well-buttered baking dish.
6. Sprinkle with onions, add a layer of chipped beef, and pour over all a layer of white sauce.
7. Add another layer of each and finish the top with a layer of potatoes and white sauce.
8. Bake in a reflector oven for about 1 hour.

Instead of preparing sauce, use concentrated, undiluted mushroom or celery soup.

LAKS LAADE   Sweden
(Salmon Casserole)

24 potatoes, sliced
butter or margarine
1½ lbs. salt salmon or 3 cans (7-8 oz.)
1½ C. bread or zwieback crumbs
salt, pepper
(be careful of salt if salt salmon is used)

1. Place alternate layers of sliced potatoes, pieces of fish, and seasoning in a buttered shallow dish.
2. Add enough water to cover.
3. Sprinkle top with zwieback or buttered bread crumbs.
4. Bake for at least 1 hour.

INDIVIDUAL PIZZAS

½ lb. salami
biscuit dough (2 C. flour or biscuit mix)
2 C. (½ lb.) grated sharp cheddar cheese
1 (6 oz.) can tomato paste
1 Tbsp. whole oregano

1. Shred salami with knife or shears.
2. Roll biscuit dough very thin.
3. Cut into 12 rounds (5½ in. in diameter).
4. Place on cookie sheet and flute edges.
5. Spread with tomato paste; sprinkle with oregano (⅛-¼ tsp. per round).
6. Top with salami and cheese.
7. Bake until biscuit is brown (15-20 minutes).

MEAT LOAF

3 lbs. ground beef
1 Tbsp. salt
½ tsp. thyme
2 C. soft bread crumbs
1 tall can (1⅔ C.) evaporated milk
tomato barbecue sauce

1. Mix all ingredients in baking pan.
2. Shape into individual loaves in shallow pan.
3. Bake 30 minutes at moderate heat (350° at home).
4. Serve with a tomato barbecue sauce, if desired.

OVEN DRUMSTICKS

2 lbs. ground beef
2 tsp. salt
2 eggs
24 soda crackers
6 slices bacon
12 skewers

1. Mix beef, salt, and eggs.
2. Divide in 12 portions.
3. Crumble soda crackers by placing in paper bag and rolling with rolling pin. Then put crumbs on wax paper.
4. Mold mixture around skewer to look like drumstick and roll in crumbs.
5. Place in shallow baking pan and bake 15 minutes in very hot oven (450° F. at home).
6. Cut bacon into halves and put on meat; bake another 15 minutes.

Crushed corn flakes or other ready-to-eat cereals may be used instead of soda crackers.

BAKED FRANKFURTERS

1 medium onion, chopped
6 Tbsp. salad oil
2 Tbsp. sugar
2 tsp. dry mustard
2 tsp. paprika
salt, pepper
1 C. catsup
1 C. water
½ C. vinegar
2 Tbsp. Worcestershire sauce
1 drop of Tabasco sauce
24 frankfurters

1. Cook onion in oil until golden.
2. Add combined remaining ingredients except frankfurters.
3. Simmer 15 minutes.
4. Split frankfurters and place cut side down in shallow baking dish.
5. Pour sauce over them.
6. Bake 30 minutes, basting several times.

GREEN PEPPERS STUFFED WITH CORN

12 green peppers
6 C. fresh corn or
3 (1 lb. 13 oz.) cans corn
1½ C. cream or milk
½ tsp. salt
¼ tsp. pepper
paprika

1. Remove tops and seeds from the green peppers.
2. Cover with boiling water, simmer 15 minutes, and drain.
3. Put in a saucepan fresh corn or drained canned corn; add cream or milk and simmer 35 minutes.
4. When cream is absorbed, add enough water or liquid from a can of corn to prevent burning.
5. Season with salt and pepper.
6. Fill peppers with the mixture.
7. Then using a muffin pan, bake in a reflector oven for ½ hour.

8. Sprinkle tops with paprika. May be served with tomato sauce (or heated concentrated tomato soup—undiluted).

GREEN PEPPERS STUFFED WITH GROUND MEAT

12 green peppers
1 C. bread crumbs
2 eggs
3 lbs. ground beef
salt, pepper
tomato catsup

1. Core and clean green peppers.
2. Mix the ground meat with bread crumbs and eggs.
3. Season and stuff the green peppers with the mixture.
4. Place the stuffed peppers in a shallow pan with a small amount of water in the bottom and bake them in a reflector oven for about ½ hour.
5. Serve with tomato catsup (or heated concentrated tomato soup—undiluted).

BAKED AVOCADO Southeastern United States

6 avocados
¼ C. butter or margarine
water or milk
3 C. dry bread crumbs
¾ tsp. salt
pepper

1. Select avocados that are just ripe (meat firm).
2. Cut in half, remove seed, and fill seed cavity with mixture of bread crumbs, seasoned and made moist with a small amount of water (or milk) butter, salt, and pepper.
3. Bake in a reflector oven until bread crumbs are brown.

SPOON BREAD Southeastern United States

2½ C. cornmeal
1¼ tsp. salt
5 C. boiling water
5 Tbsp. melted butter or margarine
5 eggs
1½ C. sweet milk
¼ C. baking powder

1. Mix cornmeal and salt.
2. Add boiling water and melted butter.
3. Beat in well-beaten eggs and milk.
4. Add baking powder.
5. Mix well.
6. Bake in deep, well-greased pans.

REFLECTOR OVEN

109

SOUR DOUGH BREAD

4 C. flour
2 Tbsp. salt
4 Tbsp. sugar
water
2 Tbsp. vinegar

1. Mix flour, salt, and sugar.
2. Add sufficient water to make a thick, creamy batter.
3. Stir in vinegar and put in a pail or bowl.
4. Let it remain in a warm place for 2 days so it can sour.

For bread: Take half of the sour dough and thicken it with more flour until it is of a consistency to knead. Knead thoroughly and work into small loaves. Place before the fire and let the loaves rise for about 1½ hours. Bake in reflector oven.

For biscuits: Add flour to ½ of the sour dough in the same way as with bread. Roll out biscuits and bake them in a reflector oven.

This sour dough is a time saver for campers. It is easy to manipulate and will supply yeast for cakes and bread. Sour dough can be kept going by adding more flour, salt, sugar, and water in proportion to the recipe as the basic supply needs replenishing. It improves with age.

CORN BREAD

4 C. yellow cornmeal
1 C. flour
1 tsp. salt
8 tsp. baking powder
2 tsp. sugar
½ C. shortening
4 C. water (approximately)

1. Combine dry ingredients and shortening.
2. Stir in the water gradually, avoiding lumps, until the mixture is just thick enough to drop from a spoon.
3. For a crisp sheet of corn bread fill the reflector pan half full. If a frying pan is used have the batter about ½ in. deep.
4. Bake 20-30 minutes until done.

SNOW BREAD

6 C. flour
2 Tbsp. cold shortening
1½ Tbsp. salt
18 C. light, fresh snow

1. Thoroughly mix flour, shortening, and salt, but be sure they are very cold. This is essential, since the whole success of the operation depends upon cold, outdoor temperature.
2. Put the ingredients together in a well-greased, cold baking pan and then add approximately 18 cups of light, fresh snow.
3. Chop and mix with a spoon or paddle until it is a crumbly mass.
4. Press down into the baking pan and bake in a hot reflector oven about ½ hour. The air in the snow takes the place of baking powder.

FOIL REFLECTOR OVEN

SNOW CORN BREAD

After a fall of light, feathery snow, superior corn bread may be made by stirring together:

1 qt. cornmeal
½ tsp. soda
1 tsp. salt
1 Tbsp. shortening
1 qt. fresh, light snow

1. Mix all ingredients except snow.
2. In a cool place where the snow has not melted, scoop up 1 qt. of light snow and combine in mixture. The snow has the same leavening effect as eggs.
3. Bake in reflector oven about 45 minutes.

PEANUT BUTTER BREAD

4 C. flour
2⅔ Tbsp. baking powder
2 tsp. salt
½ C. sugar
1⅓ C. peanut butter
2½ C. milk

1. Mix flour, baking powder, salt, and sugar.
2. Add milk to peanut butter; blend well; and add to dry ingredients.
3. Beat mixture thoroughly. The dough must be soft enough to take the shape of the pan.
4. Bake in a greased loaf pan in a reflector oven 45 to 50 minutes.
   Bread is best when a day old.

CHEESE TOAST

24 slices buttered bread
½ tsp. paprika
¾ lb. American cheese
1 tsp. Worcestershire sauce

1. Toast bread.
2. Make paste of cheese and seasonings.
3. Spread on toast and put in oven to brown (may be propped—without oven—in front of fire to brown).

BISCUITS

4 C. flour
2 Tbsp. baking powder
1 tsp. salt
½ C. shortening
1½ C. milk or water (to desired consistency)

1. Combine dry ingredients and work in shortening with knife or fingers until evenly distributed.
2. Add liquid all at once, mixing quickly until no dry flour remains.
3. Turn out on lightly floured surface and knead gently ten strokes.
4. Roll or pat dough ½ in. thick; cut in 2 in. circles.
5. Bake on ungreased sheet until golden brown.

BISCUIT MIX

9 C. flour
4½ Tbsp. baking powder
1 Tbsp. salt
¼ C. sugar
1½ C. shortening (not needing refrigeration)

1. Mix well baking powder, salt, sugar, and flour.
2. Cut in shortening until mixture resembles coarse crumbs.
3. Store in tightly covered containers.
4. Keep at room temperature.

To measure: pile mix lightly into cup and level off with knife. Makes 13 cups.

Biscuits
⅓ C. liquid (milk or water) to 1 C. mix

1. Knead and form into biscuits.
2. Bake 15 minutes.

Griddle Cakes
(makes 18)

6 C. biscuit mix
1 C. milk
2 eggs

Combine ingredients and bake on griddle.

Variations

Using the same recipe, make a biscuit about 2 in. across and flat on top. Butter the top and place a duplicate piece of dough on it. When baked the two parts will separate and may be used as a foundation for any kind of shortcake.

Roll the dough into a thin sheet and bake in one piece on a large cookie tin. Spread with jam or with applesauce to which raisins and cinnamon have been added. Cut in squares and serve.

Place a little orange marmalade or a lump of sugar dipped in orange juice in the center of each biscuit and bake.

113

CHEESE BISCUITS

3 C. flour
2 Tbsp. baking powder
1 tsp. salt
2 Tbsp. shortening
1 C. milk and water in equal parts
1 C. grated cheese

Mix and bake as described under biscuits.

MUFFINS

2 C. flour
3 tsp. baking powder
1 tsp. salt
2 Tbsp. sugar
1 egg, well-beaten
1¼ C. milk
⅓ C. salad oil

1. Mix dry ingredients.
2. Add rest all at once and stir briefly. Batter should be lumpy.
3. Fill greased muffin tins ⅔ full.
4. Bake 25-30 minutes in hot oven (400° F.).

MUFFINS (made with mix)

2 C. biscuit mix
1 egg
¾ C. milk

1. Add liquids to mix and beat to mix well.
2. Fill 12 well-greased muffin tins ⅔ full.
3. Bake 15 minutes in hot oven (400° F.).

BRAN MUFFINS

2 C. flour
2 C. bran
1 tsp. salt
5 tsp. baking powder
1½ C. milk
¼ C. melted shortening
½ C. molasses or sugar
2 eggs, well-beaten

1. Mix dry ingredients. Add milk gradually.
2. Add eggs, molasses, and melted shortening.
3. Bake in hot oven about 20 minutes. Reflector baking may take longer.

SALLY LUNN MUFFINS

3 Tbsp. butter or margarine
1 C. sugar
3 eggs
4 C. flour
4 tsp. baking powder
1⅓ C. milk

1. Cream butter and sugar.
2. Add beaten yolks of eggs.
3. Mix flour with baking powder and stir into mixture, alternating with milk.
4. Fold in well-beaten egg whites. Bake in muffin tins.

HONEY MUFFINS

2 C. honey
2 C. milk
6 eggs, beaten
6 C. flour
¼ C. baking powder
1½ tsp. salt
½ C. melted butter (or other shortening)

1. Mix honey with milk (which may be warm).
2. When they are blended, add the beaten eggs and stir in flour, which has been mixed with the baking powder and salt.
3. Stir to a batter; then add melted shortening.
4. Bake in greased muffin tins.

Berries may be added; the mixture may also be used for individual steamed fruit puddings.

BLUEBERRY MUFFINS

½ C. shortening
⅔ C. sugar
2 eggs, well-beaten
4 C. flour
1 tsp. salt
3 Tbsp. baking powder
2 C. milk
2 C. fresh blueberries

1. Cream shortening and sugar. Add beaten eggs.
2. Mix dry ingredients and add alternately with milk to creamed mixture.
3. Add berries, slightly floured.
Bake 20-25 minutes.

115

SPICE CAKE

⅓ C. shortening
1 C. sugar
2 eggs
1¾ C. flour
2½ tsp. baking powder
¼ tsp. salt
½ tsp. cinnamon
¼ tsp. cloves
¼ tsp. nutmeg
⅔ C. milk
1 tsp. vanilla

1. Cream shortening and sugar.
2. Add eggs and blend again.
3. Mix dry ingredients; add alternately with milk and vanilla to egg mixture.
4. Pour into 2 greased 8-in. pans, cupcake pans, or loaf pan.
5. Bake at 350° for 25 to 30 minutes.
6. After taking the cake from the oven, it can be dotted with semi-sweet chocolate bits which will melt from the heat of the cake.

GINGERBREAD

⅔ C. shortening
2 C. molasses
2 eggs
1 C. sour milk
3½ tsp. soda
4 tsp. cinnamon
2 tsp. ginger
1 tsp. salt
3½ C. flour

1. Heat shortening and molasses.
2. Beat eggs and sour milk.
3. Mix dry ingredients.
4. Combine mixtures and beat until smooth.
5. Pour into a shallow cake pan that has been greased and dusted with flour.
6. Bake 20 minutes in a reflector oven.

GINGERBREAD AND APPLESAUCE COBBLER

1 (14 oz.) pkg. gingerbread mix
1 (1 lb. 4 oz.) can applesauce

1. Follow directions on package for cookies.
2. Put applesauce in a baking pan and heat.
3. Dot with gingerbread cookie dough.
4. Bake in reflector oven for time listed on package.

CAKE TOPPINGS

1 C. chocolate bittersweet chips (6 oz. pkg.)
or
1 C. caramel chips (6 oz. pkg.)
or
2 milk chocolate bars (5¢ or 10¢ size)

1. Place candies or chips on top of 8 in. sq. of hot cake.
2. Let it melt and spread with knife.

OR

Top hot cake with miniature marshmallows (or quartered regular-sized ones) and put in oven again to toast marshmallows.

COFFEE CAKE

2 Tbsp. sugar
1 egg
¾ C. milk
2 C. biscuit mix

Optional

1 C. fresh berries or well-drained canned ones (wild huckleberries, blueberries, etc.)

or

1 C. cut up dates or figs

1. Combine first 4 ingredients.
2. Beat well.
3. Fold in fruit.
4. Spread in greased 9-in. round layer pan or 8- or 9-in. square pan.
5. Sprinkle with favorite topping or mix 2 tsp. cinnamon, ¼ C. sugar, 2 Tbsp. biscuit mix, 2 Tbsp. soft butter blended until crumbly for topping.
6. Bake 20-30 minutes (in 400° oven at home).

117

ONE-HUNDRED-YEAR-OLD JOHNNYCAKE

3 C. flour
3 C. fine cornmeal
1¼ tsp. salt
1 tsp. soda
3 eggs, well-beaten
1½ C. sour milk or buttermilk
1 C. sour cream

1. Combine dry ingredients.
2. Add beaten eggs, milk, and cream.
3. Mix well.
4. Put in cakepan or muffin tins and bake 30 minutes in hot oven (400°F. at home).

MARGUERITES

24 saltines
24 nutmeats
24 marshmallows (½ lb.)

1. Put a marshmallow on each saltine and place in a reflector oven pan.
2. Toast until the marshmallows brown and melt slightly.
3. Remove from heat and place a nutmeat on each marshmallow.
4. A drop of jam may be substituted for the nutmeat.

CHERRY DELIGHT

1 can cherry pie filling (2½ C.)
1½ C. flour
1 tsp. salt
1 C. brown sugar
1 C. oatmeal
1 tsp. soda
½ C. shortening

1. Blend together dry ingredients.
2. Cut in shortening.
3. Put half crumb mixture in 8x12x2 pan.
4. Pour cherry pie filling on top.
5. Cover with rest of crumbs.
6. Bake in reflector oven until crust is brown — about 20 minutes.

COBBLERS

3 C. sugar for fresh fruit (or ¾ C. sugar for canned fruit)
¾ C. flour (optional)
1½ tsp. cinnamon
6 C. canned fruit (with 2¼ C. juice)
OR
9 C. fresh fruit—cherries, peaches, berries
3 C. biscuit mix
1 C. liquid

1. Mix sugar, cinnamon, flour, and fruit (use juice if canned).
2. Divide among 3 greased 2 qt. casseroles.
3. Combine biscuit mix and liquid. Pat dough ½ in. thick.
4. Put in biscuit-sized pieces on top of fruit.
5. Bake ½ hour. Serve hot.

MOLASSES PUDDING New England

12 thick slices whole wheat bread
⅓ C. butter or margarine
4 C. milk
1¼ C. molasses

1. Spread the bread generously with creamed butter and cut in cubes.
2. Arrange in a baking dish.
3. Mix milk and molasses; reserve ½ cup and pour remainder over bread.
4. Bake in a reflector oven for 40 minutes, stirring twice during first 30 minutes; then add remaining milk and finish cooking.

COCOROONS

1 C. sugar
½ tsp. salt
2 egg whites (beaten stiff)
2 C. corn flakes
1 C. coconut, shredded or flaked
½ tsp. vanilla

1. Fold sugar and salt gradually into egg whites.
2. Fold in corn flakes and coconut.
3. Add vanilla and drop by teaspoonfuls on a greased baking sheet.
4. Bake 15 minutes in slow oven at 300 F. Yields about 3 dozen.

119

BAKED APPLES

12 large ripe apples
½ C. nutmeats
½ C. coconut, shredded
12 dates
½ C. brown sugar
12 marshmallows

1. Remove the core from the apples. Be sure not to cut through the skin at one end.
2. Fill the hole with nuts, dates, and coconut.
3. Sprinkle well with brown sugar.
4. Put in ashes or reflector oven to bake.
5. When tender, toast a marshmallow and put it on top of the apple.

BAKED APPLES WITH BANANAS

8 apples
6 bananas
1 C. sugar
9 Tbsp. butter or margarine
¾ C. boiling water

1. Slice the apples, which have been cored and pared.
2. Then peel and slice the bananas.
3. Place fruit in alternate layers in a greased baking dish, sprinkling each layer with ⅓ C. of sugar and 3 Tbsp. butter.
4. Pour the boiling water over the fruit; cover the dish closely and bake for ½ hour.
5. Remove the cover and continue the baking for 10 minutes longer.
6. Serve with the juice that forms in the baking pan. (Could be done in Dutch oven.)

POMMES AU RIZ Canada
(Apples with Rice)

1 C. water
¾ C. butter
12 large baking apples, peeled and cored
2 C. brown sugar
½ tsp. grated lemon rind
2 C. soft boiled rice
1 Tbsp. butter or margarine (for top of apples)
sweet cream, if desired

1. Heat water with butter. Do not allow to boil.
2. Butter a deep casserole and put in apples, close together.
3. Fill the centers of apples with 1½ C. of sugar mixed with lemon rind.
4. Sprinkle ¼ C. of sugar over the apples.
5. Pour the warm water and butter mixture in from the edge of the pan.
6. Cover and bake in a reflector oven for 15 to 20 minutes.
7. Mix soft boiled rice with ¼ C. of sugar and ⅔ Tbsp. of apple juice from casserole.
8. Cover apples with rice and dot with the Tbsp. of butter.
9. Cover and return to the oven and bake until apples and rice are very tender.

In some sections of Canada, all ingredients are mixed and served like a mush. In other sections, this dish is allowed to brown over the top by removing cover during the last 10 minutes. It is served hot in the casserole with heavy sweet cream.

APPLE CRISP

⅔ C. butter or margarine
16 apples, sliced (about 2 qts.)
2 tsp. cinnamon
1 C. water
2 C. sugar
1½ C. flour

1. Grease baking dish and fill with apples.
2. Add mixture of water and cinnamon.
3. Work together the remaining ingredients with the fingertips until crumbly and spread over the apple mixture.
4. Bake uncovered for about 30 minutes.
5. Serve with cream, lemon sauce, or maple sirup.

APPLE CHARLOTTE

butter or margarine
8 large apples (sliced thin)
granulated sugar
12 slices buttered bread or toast
juice of 3 lemons
juice of 3 oranges
1 C. orange marmalade

1. Butter a baking dish and put in a layer of thinly sliced apples.
2. Sprinkle with sugar — the amount depends upon the tartness of the apples — and cover with a layer of buttered bread or toast.
3. Add another layer of apples and sugar and sprinkle with mixed lemon and orange juice.
4. Use remaining bread spread liberally with orange marmalade as topping.
5. Bake for about 45 minutes in a reflector oven.

SOUTH SEA DELIGHT

12 large ripe bananas
juice of 2 large oranges
½ C. light brown sugar
½ C. coconut, shredded or flaked
½ C. fine bread crumbs

1. Peel the bananas and cut them in halves lengthwise.
2. Arrange the halves of bananas side by side in layers in a shallow buttered baking dish.
3. Mix together the juice of the oranges and brown sugar and pour over the banana layers.
4. Combine the bread crumbs and the coconut and sprinkle over the top of the bananas.
5. Bake until the bananas are tender and the coconut is brown.
6. Serve at once.

2. A WHOLE MEAL IN A HOLE

Conservation of heat and long, slow cooking are the principles of meals-in-a-hole. This technique is (or was) used in one form or another in the Islands of the Pacific; by the Ancients of the Mediterranean countries; by campers in the United States and Europe; and by New Englanders for clam bakes. Directions for preparing cooking holes are described in this chapter.

When a group wants to test its organizing skill, fire-building ability, and patience, a bean hole or imu meal will offer the chance. The main idea is to provide continuing heat over a long period of time without a continual fire. You need a shovel, a pick, canvas or burlap, a rake, and stones. Shale stones should not be used because they explode when the water in them turns to steam and expands.

BEAN HOLE

1. Dig a hole a foot wider and a foot deeper than the covered pot or Dutch oven that you plan to use (or make the hole 2 to 3 times the size of the containers).

2. Line the hole with non-exploding stones. Then lay a platform of dry logs across the hole and build a large fire on top, starting with a Basic A or tepee (see pages 12 and 45). As the fire burns down, the coals will drop in the hole.

3. Keep the fire burning 1 to 2 hours by adding kindling and fuel until the stones are very hot and there is a bed of glowing coals in the bottom of the hole.

4. When the coals and the food are ready, rake or shovel half of the coals aside.

5. Set the tightly-covered pot in the hole and pack the remaining coals around and over the pot. Keep hot stones from touching the pot or they will burn the food inside.

6. Cover the hole with damp burlap or heavy canvas and then with a layer of earth so

steam and heat cannot escape. It is the steam that helps to tenderize (or cook) the food.

7. Mark the spot with rocks.
8. Dig out the pot after the necessary cooking time (4 to 6 hours) has passed and open carefully to avoid getting dirt in the pot.

If you want beans for lunch or oatmeal for breakfast, you can enjoy the fire as a fine campfire the evening before. If it's a dinner menu you're planning, you would start on the fire at breakfast time, having dug the hole and gathered the wood the day before.

IMU

1. Dig a hole 18 in. wide and 15 in. deep.
2. Line the hole with small non-exploding stones.
3. Build a large fire on a platform of dry logs across the hole, starting with a Basic A or tepee (see pages 12 and 45). Use hardwood for a fine hot bed of coals. Keep the fire burning until the stones are very hot and there is a bed of glowing coals in the bottom of the hole (about 1 to 2 hours).
4. Burn a second or auxiliary fire beside the hole to provide extra coals as needed.
5. When the coals and food are ready, rake or shovel some of the coals from the pit.
6. Line the hot rocks and remaining coals with damp clean leaves (grape, basswood, sassafras, outside cabbage leaves, beet tops). Do not use leaves from nut trees or rhubarb plants since they are bitter.
7. Place food on leaves and cover with more damp, clean leaves. Cover with wet burlap or canvas if desired.
8. Add the rest of the hot coals and cover with 6 in. of dirt.
9. After the cooking time has elapsed, open the hole carefully to avoid getting dirt in

the food. If the right sort of leaves are not available wrap the food in wet paper towels or wet kitchen parchment paper.

PIT BARBECUING.   Although pit barbecuing is similar to imu cooking, it is done on a larger scale, requiring a whole animal carcass, a huge pit, and large quantities of wood.

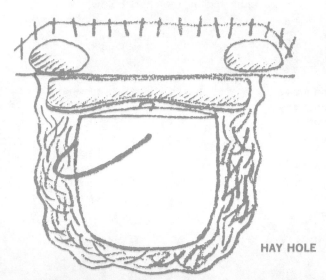

HAY HOLE

HAY HOLE

In Chapter 8 the hay box method of cooking is described. Its insulating property which is used in freezing ice cream also makes it possible to conserve heat in a hay hole. Because hay is a poor conductor of heat, the heated pot and food stay hot a long time in the hay hole. This type of fireless cooking has many advantages: the hay hole will not catch fire; fuel is saved; and the food will not burn. For these reasons the hay hole is desirable for the recipes recommended for it in this chapter as well as for selected casseroles in other chapters.

Hay holes are prepared in the following way:
1. Dig a hole a foot wider and a foot deeper than your chosen pot. Be sure the pot has a tight-fitting lid.
2. Line the hole with hay or straw, packing it tightly into a layer 6 in. thick on the bottom.

3. Prepare the food as usual, bringing it to a rapid boil before placing the covered kettle in the hole.
4. Center the tightly covered kettle in the nest of hay.
5. Pack the straw or hay around it and quickly cover it with a tightly-stuffed straw-filled sack or pillow 6 in. thick.
6. Cover the hay hole with an old piece of canvas to prevent the heat from escaping and weight its edges with stones.
7. Mark the spot when in use or empty by making a fence of sticks and twine.
8. Take food from hole when ready to serve. If necessary, reheat it.
9. It takes at least 3 times as long for anything to cook in a hay hole as over direct heat, as indicated by the chart below.

HAY HOLE TIMETABLE

	Boil Over Fire		Cook in Hay Hole
Stew	45 minutes		3 hours
Potatoes	15 minutes		2 hours
Rice	5 minutes		2½ hours
Lentils or Beans	60 minutes	plus	4 hours
Macaroni	10 minutes		2 hours
Apples	5 minutes		4 hours
Prunes	30 minutes		4 hours
Oatmeal (regular)	5 minutes		overnight

CLAM BAKES

Clam bakes, a variety of hole cookery, are seashore specialties featuring soft-shell Atlantic Coast clams or the hard-shell Pacific Coast type. See page 131 for a description of the clam bake.

CORN ROAST

A variation of the clam bake is the corn roast which is done in a shallow trench similar to the clam bake and covered with burlap or canvas. The corn silk and husks come off easily after steaming so the ear can be put into the hole well-covered in its own husk without previous husking. It adds steam if the whole ears are soaked a couple of hours in water before cooking. The pulled-back husks of cooked corn serve as a convenient handle, especially if the butt or stalk end is short. Serve corn with butter or margarine, salt and pepper. Use a brush to spread melted butter. A long shallow dish or deep narrow jar makes dipping easy.

The following recipes are for preparing food by one of the above methods. Your ingenuity and imagination will suggest variations and substitutions for the ingredients listed. Refer to the preceeding directions for details of cooking.

HAMBURGER SUPREME

3 onions
1 Tbsp. fat
3½ lbs. hamburger
10 medium potatoes, thinly sliced
salt, pepper

1. Fry onions quickly in fat in a Dutch oven or baking dish.
2. Remove most of the onions and fat and put a layer of hamburger in the oven or baking dish and season.
3. Sprinkle more of the onions and fat over the hamburger and put in a layer of sliced potatoes.
4. Alternate layers, ending with hamburger.
5. Cover tightly and cook 2 to 4 hours in a bean hole.

If the hamburger is dry and contains little fat or moisture, it will be necessary to add several tablespoonsful of water before putting Dutch oven in the bean hole.

SCALLOPED HAM WITH POTATOES AND ONIONS

4 ham slices, ½-in. thick
12 medium potatoes
3 sweet onions
salt, pepper, paprika
1 pt. milk
2 Tbsp. flour

1. Place a slice of ham in the bottom of a Dutch oven or a baking dish with a tight-fitting lid to keep the steam in.
2. Cover the ham with a layer of thinly sliced raw potatoes and then a layer of sliced onions.
3. Alternate to the top of the baking dish, making ham the top layer.
4. Season with salt, pepper, and a dash of paprika (seasoning should go over potatoes and onions).
5. Cover with milk into which the flour has been mixed.
6. Bake 2 to 4 hours in a bean hole.

HAM WITH YAMS AND PINEAPPLE

12 sweet potatoes or yams, parboiled
2 ham slices, 1-in. thick
12 slices pineapple
⅓ C. brown sugar
¼ C. butter
½ C. juice from pineapple

1. Place a layer of sliced sweet potatoes in the bottom of a greased kettle or Dutch oven.
2. Put in a slice of ham and then a layer of 6 pineapple slices.
3. Put in another slice of ham, a layer of pineapple, and a layer of sweet potatoes.
4. Sprinkle with sugar and dot with butter.
5. Add a half cup of pineapple juice for moisture.
6. Cover tightly and cook for 2 hours in a bean hole.

HAM IN A HOLE

2 ham slices, 1-in. thick
18 carrots
18 medium onions, thinly sliced
salt, pepper, prepared mustard

1. Wash and trim the ham slices.
2. Cut carrots into thin strips. Then place a layer of the carrots and a layer of onions on the bottom of a greased Dutch oven or covered baking dish.
3. Season with salt and pepper.
4. Lay one slice of the ham on onions and spread with prepared mustard.
5. Put in another layer of carrots, onions, ham, and mustard and pour in 1 C. of water.
6. Cover tightly and bake 3 to 4 hours in a bean hole.

BEAN HOLE BEANS
6 C. navy beans
2 small onions, minced
2 tsp. dry mustard
1¼ lbs. salt pork
3 tsp. salt
¼ C. brown sugar
pinch of soda
½ C. molasses

1. Wash beans and soak in water, preferably overnight.
2. Cook beans over low heat for 1 hour.
3. Grease Dutch oven or kettle and sprinkle a layer of onions on the bottom.
4. Pour in half of the beans with some of the liquid in which they were parboiled.
5. Sprinkle half of a mixture of soda, mustard, salt, and brown sugar over the beans.
6. Add a layer of diced salt pork and rest of the onions.
7. Pour in the remainder of the beans and sprinkle over this final layer the remaining dry ingredients and pork.
8. Pour the molasses over all. The beans should be just covered with liquid.
9. Place a tight-fitting lid on the kettle. It should fit securely, for the beans will dry out if the steam escapes.
10. Cook in bean hole 4-6 hours.

LIMA BEANS AND BACON
8 C. cooked large dry limas
2 C. bean cooking liquid
2 cloves garlic
½ C. finely chopped onion
1 C. chili sauce
2 Tbsp. brown sugar
8 slices bacon

1. Mix all ingredients except bacon in pot.
2. Cover with the bacon.
3. Cook in covered Dutch oven in a bean hole 4 hours.

1 C. of uncooked lima beans equals 2 C. cooked.

CLAM BAKE

1½ pk. clams
2 doz. ears of corn in the husks
4 to 5 lbs. potatoes (1 apiece)
1 lb. melted butter or margarine
4 bu. wet seaweed or rockweed

Also needed are stones, hardwood, a shovel, a scrub brush, and a bucket of fresh water.

1. Dig a hole 8 to 10 in. deep and 4 ft. square.
2. Line hole with stones.
3. Build a fire of hardwood on top of the rocks. Burn for 2 hours until it makes a bed of coals and the stones are hot.
4. While fire is burning down to coals, scrub clam shells thoroughly in fresh water. Use only those that are tightly closed around the live clam. Discard any open shells or broken ones.
5. When coals are ready, remove any burning wood that is left and cover the rocks and coals with 4 in. of wet seaweed or rockweed. Lay clams, corn, and potatoes on the weeds and cover with another layer of weeds.
6. Cover entirely with canvas and cook for 40 minutes. The clams open during cooking.
7. Serve clams, potatoes, and corn with melted butter. Using the dark neck of the clam as a handle, dip the rest of the clam in melted butter. Bite off at the neck and then just discard neck.

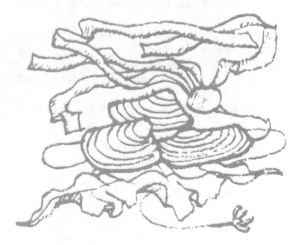

MEAL-IN-A-HOLE

4 lbs. roast beef
24 small potatoes
12 apples
12 carrots, sliced
salt, pepper

1. Wipe roast dry, season, and sear in a Dutch oven.
2. Peel potatoes, scrape and slice carrots, and core apples.
3. Season the potatoes and carrots.
4. Surround the roast with apples, potatoes, and carrots.
5. Cover tightly; cook 4 to 5 hours in bean hole.

(See Chapter 9—takes about 4 hours in a bean hole.)

CHICKEN IMU

3 chickens (2½ lbs. each)
salt
12 ears of corn in husks
12 sweet or white potatoes,
in the skin and washed

1. Clean the chickens and rub with salt but do not cut into pieces.
2. Place chicken, corn, and potatoes directly on wet leaves in pit or if there are no suitable leaves wrap food in wet paper towels or wet kitchen parchment paper.
3. Cook 2 hours in imu.

MULLIGAN STEW

(See Chapter 9—takes about 4 hours in a bean hole after boiling.)

13. EMBER COOKING

Thus far most of the recipes have relied on wood as the source of cooking heat, using either hot flame or constant coals. In order to avoid confusion with the cold black stuff in a basement coal bin, let's refer to the glowing coals of the fire as embers. These are produced more quickly from charcoal than from a stick of hardwood because "charcoal burners" have already charred the wood before the fire builder gets it.

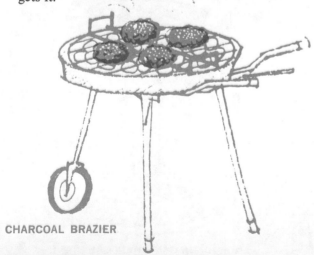

CHARCOAL BRAZIER

CHARCOAL

Charcoal is a light, clean, and porous fuel that does the work of several hardwood logs with less effort to you. Its compact size and efficiency make it effective for use in small spaces such as enclosed fireplaces or small charcoal stoves. Because it is also clean it is useful in backyard stoves and on gravel driveways, leaving no evidence afterward. Once it is started, there is no flame to blacken your pots or to escape as a fire hazard. Neither is there any smoke. You can drown hot charcoal in water to put it out and then dry it to save for another day.

Charcoal comes in special cardboard boxes, foil cartons, pre-treated quickly igniting bags, and large paper sacks. Manufacturers are always developing new packaging and improving on the type of chunks and briquets.

Charcoal burns to a bed of glowing embers

133

in 15 to 20 minutes, so plan to start the fire that much ahead of the time you want to cook on it. Since charcoal is a fuel and not tinder, it needs some easy burning starter. Use a good basic fire starting with tinder and add the charcoal—smaller pieces first—when the fire is going briskly or use starters and the puffer such as described in Chapter 4. Commercial fire starters may be fire hazards. Once the charcoal starts to burn (a grey ash appears on the pieces), other pieces may be added to the fire. Tap the pieces occasionally to remove the fine grey ash that holds in the heat. Charcoal burns from the bottom up and from the outside in. It needs a good draft especially when starting, so provide a way for air to get to it. Fire must be raised off the ground or up from the stones of a fireplace. Charcoal stoves make allowances for the draft with air vents at the bottom and also at the top so food or kettles don't block the draft.

CHARCOAL STOVES. There are several designs of "do it yourself" charcoal stoves as well as many commercially constructed ones. Choose one that is the right size for the use you want to make of it and that is appropriate for the place you want to use it. If the tin can (No. 10 size) charcoal stove is used, allow one stove for every 2 persons, otherwise cooking will take too long.

NO. 10 TIN-CAN CHARCOAL STOVE

In addition to the charcoal, the stove, and starters, you will find additional need for the following: work gloves for convenience in handling hot things around the stove; a pair of utility tongs for putting fresh charcoal on the fire, rearranging the burning coals, and dipping leftover hot coals in the water to save for a later use; and an ash plate (such as a can lid or piece of metal) as a fire safety precaution for catching ashes under the stove if the stove does not already have a built-in one.

Experience with available charcoal in your locality will give you confidence and also a chance to develop your own techniques as a charcoal cook. Charcoal provides an even heat for many of the recipes listed in other chapters of the book, especially the ones cooked in aluminum foil (see Chapter 13).

Foods can be cooked directly on embers. Some foods are protected from direct contact with the hot embers by their own skin (banana boats and baked eggs); by rock salt or sand (baked potatoes in sand or salt); by a crust that cooks on (steak cooked on the coals); or by aluminum foil (Lyonnaise potatoes).

FOIL COOKING

A cook who wants to foil toil in her outdoor kitchen could use the same product that's popular in home kitchens—aluminum foil—but she had better get the heavy weight that's usually designated for freezer use. The thinner type works fine for wrapping sandwiches or leftovers but doesn't provide enough protection against punctures or extreme heat.

When foil is wrapped as an airtight package around food, finishing off with a drugstore or sandwich fold, it becomes a small-scale pressure cooker. When placed in a bed of hot coals with some heat on top, diced vegetables and meat cook in 10 to 15 minutes in this package, and whole potatoes in 40 to 50 minutes. Be

135

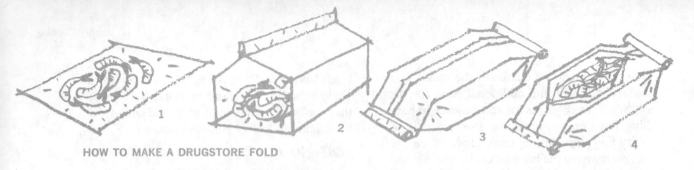

sure to allow some space for expansion in the package by not wrapping the raw food too tightly. If you want food to brown or to broil as in a skillet, leave the package open at the top (or fashion like a folded drinking cup with a flat bottom). This allows the steam to escape and makes it possible for you to watch the progress too.

Using individual foil packages—closed or open—is a clean convenient way in which to prepare food at home, to carry it, to cook it, and eat it—all in a single container which can be disposed of in a trash can or crushed and carried home with you. You will find the foil package desirable when cooking in city parks or in someone's backyard. It also allows for individual taste preferences—pepper, onions or whatever you choose. It makes no difference whether the shiny side of the foil is on the inside or the outside.

For turning and removing hot foil packets from the fire use a shovel or utility tongs and/or work gloves or use two blunt sticks like oversize chopsticks. But be careful not to poke holes in the foil through which steam or juice escapes and dirt gets in. Once safely out of the fire, make holes on top of the packet to let dangerous steam escape before you start to open the top. Then you are ready to eat out of your aluminum foil cooking dish. Foil cooking is a technique for experienced cooks who know how to handle fire, heat, and steam pressure safely.

Foil also has other outdoor uses: as an improvised reflector oven; as a windbreak; as a means of concentrating the heat of a fire; as improvised utensils on a forked stick (as saucepan or skillet). Foil is also effectively used for making the end of a dubious toasting fork both clean and fireproof. Just wrap the fork end in foil before the food is impaled. If food requires a greased pan at home in the kitchen, grease the aluminum inside before putting the food in. When foil is handled with care it can be washed and reused after being flattened out again.

EMBER VARIATIONS

Another way to cook a "meal in one" on the embers is "stew in a coffee can" (vacuum-pack type). The top fits tightly enough to keep the steam in and to produce a slight head of steam. It too is a small pressure cooker.

It is also possible to cook right on or above the embers in an orange shell and in containers of sand, rock salt, banana peels or apple skin.

When you read the following recipes check the necessary equipment and be sure to have a successful substitute on hand. You will find all the ones using foil listed together.

FOIL FRYING PAN

137

The recipes in this chapter are for the more experienced cook, since they require skill in using such equipment as coffee cans, aluminum foil, etc. Ingredients and equipment for all the recipes are for 12 persons. Part of the fun in preparing many of these recipes, however, is that the type of required equipment makes it feasible for each individual or every 2 persons to prepare their own food. Preparation steps for such recipes are, therefore, for 1 or 2 servings and are so indicated.

Try these recipes; then use your ingenuity to make up your own recipes.

COFFEE CAN COOKING

Basic Equipment:

6 coffee cans and lids
(1 lb. size, vacuum pack type)
6 jackknives
12 spoons

COFFEE CAN STEW

6 carrots
12 stalks of celery
12 strips of bacon
3 lbs. ground beef
6 medium size potatoes
6 onions, sliced
6 medium size tomatoes
salt, pepper
3 small green peppers

For 2 servings:

At home

1. Wash, peel, and cut 1 carrot in half and lengthwise; cut 2 celery stalks in 2-in. pieces and cut 2 bacon strips in half.
2. Mold ½ lb. of beef into 2 meat patties; slice 1 onion, 1 potato, and 1 tomato.
3. Place 2 pieces of bacon on bottom of can; add layer of onion, ground beef, more onions, pepper, tomatoes, celery, potatoes, carrots, more onions, and salt and pepper, etc.

4. If can is not full, place enough crinkled wax paper to fill balance of coffee can and close. Label on strip of masking tape to show name and/or contents of can.

On the site

1. Build fire and let it burn to embers.
2. Remove wax paper from can; place closed coffee can on embers for 25 minutes (open lid and check in 10 minutes).
3. If it seems to be browning too rapidly, pour 2 Tbsp. of water in can.

CHICKEN AND DUMPLINGS

6 broiler chickens (1½ lbs. each)
12 medium potatoes
6 Tbsp. butter or margarine
3 C. biscuit mix
6 medium carrots
12 celery stalks
1 Tbsp. salt
8 Tbsp. water
See page 138 for equipment

For 2 servings:

1. Cut half a chicken into pieces to fit can; add 1 potato, peeled and diced, on top of chicken; add ½ tsp. salt.
2. Scrape and slice 1 carrot very thin over the potatoes; cut 2 celery stalks in small pieces; pour ½ C. of water over all.
3. Mix ½ C. biscuit mix with 4 tsp. water. Then pat out 1-in. balls of dough and put on top of vegetables—as many can will hold.
4. Cover securely.
5. Place on embers and cook 1 hour.

KRAUT AND SPARERIBS

6 (14 oz.) cans sauerkraut
3 lbs. spareribs
12 medium potatoes
6 Tbsp. butter or margarine
6 medium onions
1 Tbsp. salt

See page 138 for equipment

For 2 servings:

1. Put 1 can drained kraut in the bottom of the coffee can.
2. Cut ½ lb. spareribs to fit over kraut; peel 2 potatoes and slice into ¼ in. slices over the ribs. Cut one onion fine on top of the potatoes.
3. Add 1 Tbsp. butter or margarine (or bacon fat if desired) and ½ tsp. salt.
4. Place lid on securely; put can in embers with coals part way up its side.
5. Cook at least 1 hour. Be sure pork is well done. Do not eat pink pork.

PORK CHOPS

For 2 servings:

2 thin pork chops (4 oz. each)
other ingredients as in kraut and spareribs recipe

1. Substitute pork chops for spareribs.
2. Cook 1 hour.
3. Be sure pork is well done. Do not eat pink pork.

VEAL CHOPS OR CUTLETS

For 2 servings:

2 thin veal chops or cutlets (4 oz. each)
other ingredients as in kraut and spareribs recipe

1. Substitute veal for spareribs in kraut and sparerib recipe.
2. Cook 1 hour.

SWEET POTATO CASSEROLES

(see Chapter 11—takes 1 hour in the embers)

140

POTATOES BAKED IN TIN CANS

Basic Equipment:

2 or 3 No. 10 cans
damp sand

Clean rock salt (such as used in making ice cream) may be substituted for damp sand. When using rock salt it is not necessary to salt potatoes when serving them. It is also possible to use hot pine pitch in which to cook potatoes. The pine pitch forms a crust on the potato; just break it open and eat the potato inside.

Ingredients:

12 medium potatoes
salt, pepper
¼-½ lb. butter or margarine

1. Fill cans half way with damp, clean sand or earth.
2. Bury potatoes in damp sand so they do not touch the can or each other.
3. Put tin covers on top of cans; place in fire and cook for 45 minutes or until potatoes are soft.
4. Serve potatoes in their jackets with salt, pepper, and butter.

As an alternative, potatoes may be wrapped in wet newspaper, paper towels, wax paper, or even mud and baked in hot coals. A wrapping of wax paper makes the potato softer and moistens the skin.

141

BAKING IN THE EMBERS

BAKED EGGS IN THE SHELL

12 eggs
salt, pepper
For 1 serving:

1. Pierce small end of an egg with a pin.
2. Place egg in hot ashes with small end up and bake for 10 to 20 minutes.
3. If desired, serve on hot buttered toast after seasoning with salt and pepper. (Heat seals the opening but hole allows for first steam to escape and prevents egg from bursting.

BANANA BOATS

12 bananas
12 marshmallows (about ¼ lb.)
12 small pieces milk chocolate—2 (1½ oz. bars)

For 1 serving:

1. Peel back a long strip of banana peel on the inside of the curve, leaving one end attached to the banana.
2. Scoop out some of the banana and fill with marshmallow, chocolate (and raisins).
3. Replace the strip of peeling.
4. Bake in the embers (about 15 to 20 minutes) until banana, chocolate, and marshmallow are melted and blended. It is also possible to wrap banana boats in foil.

BAKED APPLES

(see Chapter 11)

142

BAKING IN FOIL

Basic Equipment:
heavy duty aluminum foil
utility tongs
work gloves

SHRIMP BARBECUE

4 lbs. large green shrimp
1 C. butter or margarine
1 large clove garlic, minced
½ tsp. black pepper, coarsely ground
1 tsp. salt
1 C. parsley, minced

1. Peel and clean shrimp.
2. Cream butter; add remaining ingredients to the butter and mix well.
3. Cut 6 9-in. strips of heavy duty aluminum foil. Then cut each strip in half.
4. Divide shrimp equally on each piece of foil.
5. Top each with ½12 of the butter mixture; bring foil up around shrimp; twist tightly to seal.
6. Place shrimp packet on embers.
7. Cook 5 minutes.

STUFFED TROUT

12 medium trout
salt, pepper
3 medium onions, chopped fine
¼ lb. butter or margarine

1. Clean the fish thoroughly; salt and pepper the insides.
2. Fill each fish about ¾ full with onion and put a pat of butter on the top of the onion.
3. Wrap each fish separately in aluminum foil.
4. Bury in hot embers. Bake 20 to 25 minutes.

FILLET OF FISH

(see *Fish in a Bag* on page 148)

1. Wrap individual portions of fish fillet in aluminum foil and season with salt and lemon juice, and butter or margarine if desired.
2. Cook in embers 10 to 12 minutes.

143

HAMBURGER DINNER

12 potatoes
12 carrots
3 lbs. hamburger
salt, pepper
See page 143 for equipment

For 1 serving:

1. Cut up potato in small pieces.
2. Cut carrot into sticks.
3. Make a pat of ¼ lb. hamburger, ¾ of an inch thick.
4. Place the ingredients side by side on a piece of aluminum foil.
5. Season; wrap in foil and put packet in the embers.
6. Cook 10 to 20 minutes.

   Other combinations can be used, such as:

   Ham, pineapple, and sweet-potatoes.
   Chicken legs, onions, and potatoes.
   Hot dogs and onions.
   Hot dogs with cheese and bacon.
   Hot dogs with apples and cheese.

BEEF STEW

3 lbs. beef cut in 1-in. chunks
12 bacon slices (about ¾ lb.)
12 tomatoes
6 onions
See page 143 for equipment

For 1 serving:

1. Place ¼ lb. of beef, 1 slice of bacon cut in pieces, slices of ½ onion and quarters of 1 tomato in aluminum foil packet.
2. Cook in embers 30 to 40 minutes.

PIGS IN BLANKETS

(see Chapter 10—takes 15 minutes wrapped in foil in the embers)
See page 143 for equipment

When cooked in the embers, pigs in blankets are known as "coal-dogs."

CORN ON THE COB

12 ears of corn
See page 143 for equipment

1. Wrap each husked ear of corn in foil.
2. Cook in embers 10 to 20 minutes.

144

STEAMED CANNED CORN AND BACON

6 cups canned corn or 4 (12 oz.) cans
6 slices bacon, diced
See page 143 for equipment

For 1 serving:

Wrap ½ C. corn and ½ slice diced bacon in foil and cook in embers 5 minutes.

LYONNAISE POTATOES

12 medium potatoes
12 small onions
See page 143 for equipment

For 1 serving:

1. Cut 1 large potato and 1 onion into thin slices.
2. Mix and wrap in foil with a little salt and butter.
3. Put in embers to cook for 15 minutes.

STUFFED PEPPERS

(see Chapter 11)

See page 143 for equipment

POTATO—ONIONS

12 medium potatoes
6 medium mild onions, sliced in rounds
¼ lb. butter or margarine
salt, pepper
See page 143 for equipment

For 1 serving:

1. Cut potato in 4 crosswise slices.
2. Spread butter on each side of the slices.
3. Cut ½ onion in rounds and place between potato slices; salt and pepper them.
4. Secure slices with toothpicks or skewers.
5. Wrap these potato-onions tightly in foil.
6. Bake in embers 30 to 40 minutes.

SUBMARINE (HERO) SANDWICHES

See page 143 for equipment

Wrap your favorite submarine sandwich (made on a long hard roll or French bread with your favorite filling) in aluminum foil and heat at the edge of the embers for 10 minutes.

145

GARLIC FRENCH BREAD

4 loaves French bread
1 to 2 tsp. garlic salt
2 C. butter or margarine
See page 143 for equipment

1. Melt butter and add garlic salt.
2. Use baker's French bread sliced at an angle.
3. Brush with garlic and butter in the slashes.
4. Wrap each loaf in aluminum foil and warm at the edge of the fire—not in the embers.

BISCUITS

See page 143 for equipment

May be cooked in open packet of aluminum foil. When the biscuits cook brown on one side, remove the foil and turn them over to brown on the other. Approximate time: 10 to 15 minutes.

CAKE

(use mixes—see Chapter 11)
See page 143 for equipment

Place batter in a handmade foil pan with a lid at an angle to be used as a reflector.

APPLE DELIGHT

12 large apples
4 Tbsp. sugar
¾ C. biscuit mix
½ C. raisins
3 Tbsp. cinnamon (or to taste)
See page 143 for equipment

For 1 serving:

1. Core and chop 1 apple in fairly large pieces, peeling if desired.
2. Mix 1 tsp. sugar, a few raisins and cinnamon to taste with 1 Tbsp. biscuit mix; stir into chopped apple.
3. Wrap in a piece of greased aluminum foil, leaving sufficient space for steam.
4. Cook in the embers approximately 30 to 45 minutes. (The juice of the apple moistens the dough sufficiently.)

BAKED APPLE

(See Chapter 11)
See page 143 for equipment

APPLE COBBLER

4 C. apples, sliced
1⅓ C. sugar
1 tsp. cinnamon
2 C. biscuit mix (or pie crust mix)
2 8-in. pie pans
See page 143 for equipment

1. Mix sugar and cinnamon with sliced apples and cook in saucepan until apples are tender. (Canned apple slices can be used instead.)
2. Put cooked apples in shallow pie pans.
3. Prepare dough from biscuit or pie crust mix and roll it with a round jar or small log between two pieces of wax paper.
4. Place a circle of dough on the pie filling.
5. Set on a sheet of foil, leaving half of foil exposed.
6. Fold exposed portion on three edges up and over the pie pan to form a small oven.
7. Set either on the ground or on rocks before a hot blazing fire. The portion of the pie *under the foil* will brown first from reflected heat.
8. Turn pie within the foil oven to brown evenly.
9. Bake 15 to 20 minutes.

A 2-crust pie may be made by setting 3 rocks to form a triangle. Fill triangle with live coals from fire and place pie pan on the rocks.)

BAKED BANANA

12 bananas
See page 143 for equipment

1. Wrap banana, skin and all, in a piece of foil.
2. Bake in hot embers 10 minutes.

BANANA BOATS
(see page 142)
See page 143 for equipment

147

STUFFED ONIONS

6 large onions
2 lbs. hamburger
1 egg
dash pepper
½ tsp. salt

1. Mix hamburger, egg, salt, and pepper (add other spices as desired).
2. Cut onions in half and scoop out the center of the onion half.
3. Fill the onion shells with hamburger mix.
4. Set the onion shells carefully in the embers and bake about 15-20 minutes.

It is also possible to wrap onion shells in foil.

INDIVIDUAL PUDDING CAKES

(makes 8 individual cupcakes)

1 12½-oz. pkg. muffin mix
1 C. brown sugar
1½ C. hot water
½ C. milk
¼ C. cocoa
8 tuna cans or individual muffin pans

1. Lightly grease 8 individual muffin tins or tuna cans.
2. Stir together muffin mix and milk, just until mix is moistened.
3. Divide between pans.
4. Mix sugar and cocoa; sprinkle evenly on batter.
5. Set pans carefully among the embers.
6. Pour hot water carefully on batter. (Do not stir.)
7. Bake about 20 minutes.

Individual ovens can be made by covering each cupcake pan with a larger tin.

14. GIMMICKS AND GADGETS

Once you have successfully mastered quick kettle cooking, then simple toasting and baking, you will want to experiment with unusual or unexpected ways to cook food outdoors. These include ember cooking (Chapter 13), pit cooking (Chapter 12), and other utensil-less dishes. The rule still holds: don't cook everything; have some things ready to eat. Then you won't go hungry if the pioneer drumstick plops into the fire or your main course catches fire on an errant flame.

The directions, recipes, and illustrations in this chapter are meant to be used by experienced outdoor cooks. They are only guides and are not as simple to follow as the recipes for the beginner. Timing will depend upon your own skill as a fireman and cook. Experiment and make your own additions in the book as to the timing. Some of the techniques and methods in earlier chapters can be experimented with to devise your own "specialty of the camp," new equipment designs, new taste and texture combinations, and old favorites in new guises.

All sorts of materials lend themselves to use for cooking utensils, for dishwashing, and for food storage: coat hangers, orange shells, coffee cans (Chapter 13), flat rocks (not shale), green sticks, coconut shells, aluminum foil (Chapter 13), tin cans, assorted sizes of paper bags (2-, 3-, or 5-pound sizes), empty frozen cherry cans, large clamp paper clips, metal mesh or hardware cloth. Use blank page in back of the book for sketching the designs of your own gimmicks and gadgets.

Tin-can stoves are designed for at least 3 types of heat source—Buddy burners for emergency heat when other fuel is not available or allowed; small fires made with tinder and small twigs; and charcoal fires (see Chapter 13). The small fire (made with natural fuel) needs 2 people—1 to feed the fire, the other to do the cooking.

1. Select an empty tuna can.

2. Roll a corrugated cardboard strip into a coil that fits loosely into the can. Cardboard should be ¼ in. wider than the depth of can.

3. Pour hot paraffin to fill the tuna can and let it harden.

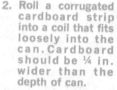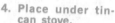

4. Place under tin-can stove.

Cooking with tin-can stoves enables you to observe the conservation rules prohibiting the cutting of green sticks. Remember that successful fire building requires:

1. Quickly ignited tinder followed by larger pieces of wood and fuel.
2. Space for air to circulate upward.

In addition to these gadgets for cooking, there are some that are designed for the cook's comfort, such as aprons, camp chaps, and pot holders. Use denim, canvas, and the ever-present bandanna. The old-fashioned red or blue (work) handkerchief is a versatile piece of cloth "as is." It can be used as a place mat or center piece, a hand towel, a "sit-upon," an apron tucked in your waistband, a rolled or folded hat, a kerchief, a pot holder, or a lunch bag. By using a piece of thread, a needle, and cord you can also convert it into a draw string ditty bag or lunch bag, a permanent apron or a blouse.

For heavy duty aprons or camp chaps, use denim. Add pockets or straps to fit your favorite utensils, such as pot holders, gloves, spoon, fork, or tongs.

Create, invent, build, and be ingenious when you cook outdoors.

Methods for utensil-less cooking include the imu in Chapter 12 and some recipes in Chapter 13. If you are where flat, smooth rocks (not shale) are available, try cooking on them. Use fairly clean and smooth ones. Heat them thor-

oughly in a hot fire, remove from fire and brush off with grass or leaves. Then they are ready to be your skillet. Work quickly in placing food on them to avoid wasting their heat.

A successful gadget is

- useful—doing its job well
- durable—lasting for reuse
- portable—easily packed and carried
- simple—easily assembled of available material
- economical—homemade, custom made, or ready made to best do its job

151

The recipes in this chapter are for the more experienced cook, since they require skill in using such equipment as orange shells and heated rocks. Ingredients and equipment for all the recipes are for 12 persons. Part of the fun in preparing these recipes, however, is that the type of required equipment makes it feasible for each individual or every 2 persons to prepare their own food. Preparation steps for the recipes are, therefore, for 1 or 2 servings and are so indicated.

Try these recipes; then use your own ingenuity to make up your own recipes.

COOKING ON ROCKS

CIRCLED EGGS

12 eggs
¼ C. shortening or bacon grease
12 rocks
12 green sticks, peeled and flexible

For 1 serving:
1. A small freshly peeled stick may be made into a circle and laid on the greased heated rock.
2. Drop the egg into the circle.
3. Allow it to cook fast to the stick, then turn it with the stick.

BACON AN' EGG ON A ROCK
(See illustration on page 153.)
36-48 slices bacon (1¾ -2½ lbs.)
12 eggs
12 rocks

For 1 serving:
1. Place 3 or 4 slices of bacon on the heated rock to form a triangle or square.
2. When these are cooked and have covered the rock with grease, break an egg in the center of the square or triangle and allow it to fry.
3. The egg will cling to the slices of bacon. If preferred, the eggs may be turned.

EGGS IN A HOLE
(See chapter tab.)
24 bacon slices (about 1¼-2½ lbs.)
12 eggs
12 slices of bread
12 rocks

For 1 serving:

1. Place 2-4 bacon slices on a heated rock.
2. When bacon is cooked on one side, turn over.
3. Remove center from a slice of bread and lay the bread on crisp sides of 2 bacon slices so that the bacon is just under the hole in the bread.
4. Break egg into the hole in the bread and lay any remaining pieces of bacon on top of the egg, crisp side down.
5. When done on one side, turn over. The egg will cling to the bread and the bacon, forming a sandwich with the bacon on the outside and the egg on the inside.

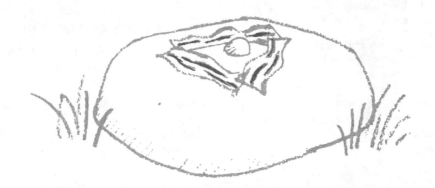

COOKING IN ORANGE SHELL

After you have eaten the pulp from half an orange, save the shell cup to use as a utensil for eggs, vegetables, or cake. Label the individual orange shells with marking pencil if you like. Be sure to remove any membrane that may have been left.

ORANGE SWEET POTATOES

6 oranges
6 C. canned sweet potatoes
¾ C. brown sugar
12 marshmallows (¼ lb.)

1. Cut oranges in half and eat pulp (or save half-shells from an earlier meal). Write names on the shell with a magic marker.
2. Mash canned sweet potatoes.
3. Pack potatoes into orange shells.
4. Sprinkle with a little brown sugar and top with marshmallows.
5. Bake in the embers.

BREAKFAST EGG

12 eggs
6 oranges
12 slices bacon (if desired)
salt, pepper

For each serving:

1. Cut orange in half, remove pulp, eat it, and save 1 half-shell.
2. Break an egg into the shell; season with salt and pepper. Set it in the coals to bake.

The shell may be lined with wax paper or bacon.

ORANGE GINGERBREAD

1 (14½ oz.) pkg. gingerbread mix
water for mix
12 orange half-shells

1. Make gingerbread mix batter. (Follow directions on package.)
2. Half fill empty orange shells with batter.
3. Cook in embers.

154

COOKING IN A CAN

If you want containers other than orange shells for eggs, use small tin cans.

VIENNA EGGS

6 small (8 oz.) cans Vienna sausages
12 empty tuna fish cans (7 oz.)
12 eggs

For 2 servings:

1. Divide 1 can of sausages including the juice between 2 tuna fish cans.
2. Nest an egg in the middle of each.
3. Put foil over the top to keep the ashes out.
4. Cook in the embers about 5 minutes.
5. Eat directly from hot cans.

EGGS ON A STICK

12 eggs
12 thin peeled green sticks, 2 ft. long

For each serving:

1. Prick holes in each end of 1 egg.
2. Insert a stick in one end and work it gently through egg and out the other end.
3. Hold both ends of stick to suspend egg over embers of small fire.
4. Turn occasionally for 10-15 minutes.
5. Eat from shell or in dish, depending on how well-done you get (or like) your egg.

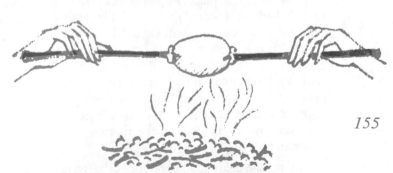

A CARDBOARD BOX OVEN

Don't throw away that sturdy carton! It will be ideal for girls to use in making a cardboard camp oven. Here's how to make one.

Cut away the top and bottom of any sturdy cardboard carton, approximately 14″ x 16″ x 14″ deep. Cover all exposed cardboard surfaces with heavy-duty aluminum foil. Cut a piece of plastic roasting wrap large enough to cover the top of the box. Fasten it securely over the top with string or wire.

To use the oven, place the pan, with the food to be baked, on a footed grill over a pan of lit charcoal briquets. The grill should be raised about 10 inches above the charcoal. Set the cardboard oven over the food and the charcoal. Prop up one end of the oven with a pebble to provide the air charcoal needs to burn—or cut air vents along the lower edge of the oven. Watch the food bake through the transparent top.

Control the baking temperature of the oven by the number of charcoal briquets used. Each briquet supplies 40 degrees of heat (a 360-degree temperature will take nine briquets).

Experiment. Build an oven to fit your pans—or your menu. • Construct a removable oven top or oven door. • Punch holes on opposite sides of the oven and run coat hanger wire through to make a grill to hold baking pans. • Figure out a way to make a collapsible oven for easy carrying. • Try the oven over the coals of a campfire or use buddy burners for fuel. • Bake bread, roast a chicken, make a meat loaf, create a pizza pie, or concoct a breakfast coffee cake.

15. EDIBLE WILD FOODS

Native foods include both wild and cultivated types. Of course, we are more familiar with the latter. As the result of modern commercial food distribution we find such native foods as mustard greens, dandelion greens, wild rice, black walnuts, blueberries, and mushrooms in our vegetable and fruit stores. Less familiar, because we must hunt for our own, are many that were used regularly by the Indians and our pioneer ancestors and are still well known by modern-day cooks who know where to find them: marsh marigold (cowslip) greens, poke salad, lamb's quarters, fiddleheads (brake fern, bracken, sensitive fern), staghorn, sumac's "pink lemonade," etc. Gourmets praise the mushroom but only the expert naturalist tries to distinguish between the edible wild ones and the disastrously poisonous wild ones.

Heed these rules when picking wild foods:

1. Be conserving; pick only those plants that: are abundant; are weeds; are not protected by local laws; are still able to grow; are not more desirable as plants than as food; are growing where you have permission to pick; and are useful, desirable, and needed for food.

2. Be safe. Pick plants that: you recognize and know are safe for eating; you know how to prepare for eating.

3. Avoid plants that: you do not recognize; do not know how to prepare. Also, avoid plants that you know to be unpalatable though edible; plants you know to be dangerous or poisonous, such as jimson weed, moonseed, buttercup, poison hemlock, water hemlock and other plants of the wild carrot family (Queen Ann's lace), white hellebore, and plants growing in soil or water that is or may be contaminated.

4. Know your mushrooms very well or avoid eating them. Consult a specialist to learn

about the many varieties. There is no simple test for finding edible ones and spotting the various poisonous ones.

5. Know your plants. Do not trust old sayings such as "humans can eat what monkeys eat in the tropics," "humans can drink any water a horse can drink," "there are no poisonous plants in Alaska." Many of these sayings are not foolproof.

Since wild food crops and their seasons vary across the country, those suggested here are only some of the many palatable plants you may find in your area. A local naturalist can help you identify many more and help you find the ones you want to eat. Many State Agricultural Extension Service offices have printed material to help you, and libraries may have the resources listed in the Bibliography. Nature trails in camps and parks may label plants that are edible and those that are not. The botanical names in the list are to help you be sure you have the right plant, since "common" names are not universally applied to the same plant everywhere. Budding botanists and Latin students will find them interesting. A nature consultant will find them useful.

These recipes are planned to show you ways to use groups of wild foods. Many will seem familiar to you who read regular cookbooks. A menu using both wild and familiar foods is more appealing than one made up of only wild foods. For example, add a soup, salad, cooked green vegetable or beverage of wild food to a regular menu, rather than making a total menu of wild foods. Experienced campers and outdoor cooks of native foods might like to try a "survival meal or weekend" in localities where these edible plants are found.

COOKED GREENS

Use any one of these or a combination (especially if green is peppery in flavor): watercress, dandelion, common chickweed, lamb's quarters, purslane, common plantain, marsh marigold, milkweed, chicory, pigweed, etc.). Use tender leaves or young shoots and boil in salted water. Serve with butter or margarine, lemon or vinegar, or other sauces familiar to the dining room.

ASPARAGUS ALTERNATES

Use fiddleheads of brake fern, sensitive fern and bracken; young shoots of milkweed; cattail (peeled); pokeweed (4-in. shoots,, avoid poisonous roots). Boil in salted water as with asparagus; serve hot with butter or margarine or favorite asparagus sauce (lemon or cheese) or in cream or white sauce. It may be necessary to discard the first water when it comes to a boil and to put the shoots in fresh water and boil again to remove strong flavor of plants such as pokeweed.

GREEN SALADS

Ingredients consist of any combination of wild greens—purslane, watercress, wild mustard, dandelions. The method of preparation is the familiar one for tossed salad: washing the greens, draining, tearing into smaller sized pieces, covering with favorite dressing (French, mayonnaise, or hot bacon dressing — especially for dandelions).

159

SOUPS

Add a handful of chopped watercress or fern fiddleheads to creamed soup made according to directions on package of dried soup or can of condensed soup.

WILD RICE

Follow directions in cookbooks. Wild rice takes longer to cook to tenderness than regular commercial white or brown rice.

ELDERFLOWER PANCAKES

Wash, shake dry, and strip flowerettes of the common elder (avoid red-berried elder); add a handful to pancake batter and cook pancakes as usual.

FRUITS AND NUTS

Fruits and nuts are familiar in the wild or cultivated form. The wild ones are used in familiar ways—as strawberry jam, in blueberry muffins and walnut cake, etc.

WILD FRUIT JELLY

For fruits with natural pectin, such as grapes, currants, and European barberry, follow the jelly recipes in kitchen cookbooks. For fruits low in pectin, such as strawberries, raspberries, and plums, use commercial pectins (powdered or liquid) and follow directions on the package.

PINK LEMONADES

Sort the berries of staghorn sumac (smooth sumac or mountain sumac), European barberry, mountain ash, or red mulberry. Discard the undesirable berries. Then place a handful of sumac berries in a clean cloth and tie loosely; boil in water until water is well colored; sweeten; serve hot or cold. With barberry, mountain ash berries or mulberries: crush; tie in clean cloth; steep in boiling hot (not actively boiling) water until it is well colored; sweeten; chill before serving.

(HOT) TEA

Many local tea flavors were known during the Revolutionary War, pioneering days, and the Civil War, so here is a chance to learn how history tasted in those days.

Use leaves from spearmint, wild strawberry, black birch, Sassafras, spice bush, or wintergreen. To a cup of boiling water add 1 tsp. of fresh leaves or ½ tsp. of dried leaves; steep 5 minutes. Serve hot, with sugar if desired. Dried black birch twigs and bark can be used in the same way.

The bark of the Sassafras root also yields a flavorsome tea. For 3 qts. of tea use the bark from a piece of root measuring 4 in. x 1 in. and boil about 15 minutes.

To dry leaves for future use, place in shady well-ventilated spot and dry quickly. When thoroughly dry, store in airtight containers.

EDIBLE PLANTS AND THEIR USES

The plants on the following list are found in the wild form but may also be familiar in the cultivated form. Check these plants to see if they grow in your locality and use them for the recipes in this chapter and elsewhere in the book (see Index).

It is important to recognize plants before attempting to eat any part of them. Avoid any you do not recognize. Of the infinite variety of plants found throughout the United States, many are either unpalatable or poisonous. Therefore, make it a rule to avoid unfamiliar plants when you go into the woods.

Plant	Botanical Name	Edible Parts & Uses
Black (sweet) Birch	*Betula lenta*	Young twigs, root bark, dried leaves —tea.
Barberry, European (common)	*Berberis vulgaris*	Sprigs of berries—preserves, jams, jelly, etc.
Barrel Cactus	Many species	Whole plant—holds water.

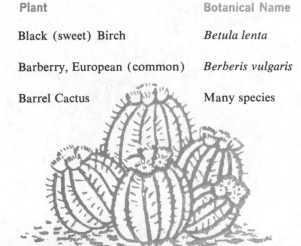

Plant	Botanical Name	Edible Parts & Uses
Beechnuts	*Fagus grandifolia*	Nut meat—raw or toasted (salted), in baking, etc.
Biscuit Root	*Lomatium geyfri*—or *Lomatium farinosum*	Fleshy roots—raw or cooked like potatoes.
Blackberries	*Rubus* (sp)	Fruit—raw, jam or preserves, cobblers, etc.
Black Walnuts	*Juglans nigra*	Nut meat—raw or toasted (salted), in baking, etc.
Blueberries	*Vaccinium* (sp)	Fruit—raw, jam, muffins, pies, cobblers, pancakes, etc.
Butternuts	*Juglans* (sp)	Nut meat—raw, toasted, in baking, etc.
Cattails (Broad Leaf)	*Typha* (sp)	Young shoots—peeled, cook like asparagus. Roots—roasted or boiled like potatoes.
Cherry (Pin, Choke, Wild, Black)	*Prunus* (sp)	Fruit—jelly.
Chestnut	*Castanea* (sp)	Nut meat—raw, toasted, in cakes, etc.
Chicory	*Chicorium intybus*	Young leaves—salads, cooked greens.

163

Plant	Botanical Name	Edible Parts & Uses
Chickweed	*Stellaria media*	Leaves—cooked greens
Cranberries	*Vaccinium* (sp)	Fruit—jams, relishes, jelly, etc.
Currants	*Ribes* (sp)	Fruit—jelly, etc.
Dandelions	*Taraxacum officinale*	Leaves—salads, cooked greens.
Dewberries	*Rubus villosus*	Fruit—raw, jam, etc.
Elderberries (Common)	*Sambucus canadensis*	Fruit—raw, jelly, etc. Flowerlets—in pancakes, waffles, etc.
Fiddleheads Brake Fern or Bracken Sensitive Fern	*Pteris aquilina* *Onoclea sensibilis*	Young shoots, woolly covering, leafy tip and lower stem removed—like asparagus.
Gooseberries	*Ribes* (sp)	Fruit—sauce, jam.
Grapes	*Vitis* (sp)	Fruit—jam, jelly, etc.
Hazelnuts	*Corylus* (sp)	Nut meat—raw, toasted, in baking, etc.
Hickory Nuts	*Carya* (sp)	Nut meat—raw, toasted, in baking, etc.
Huckleberries	*Gaylussacia* (sp)	Fruit—raw, jam, muffins, pancakes, etc.
Lamb's quarters (Pigweed)	*Chenopodium album*	Leaves from plants under 8 in. tall —cooked greens.
Manzanita	*Arctostaphylos manzanita*	Berries—stewed and sweetened.

Plant	Botanical Name	Edible Parts & Uses
Marsh Marigold (Cowslip)	*Caltha palustris*	Young leaves and stems—cooked greens.
Milkweed	*Asclepias* (sp)	Young shoots (under 8 in.)—like asparagus. Green young flower buds—cooked greens.
Miner's Lettuce	*Montia paryiflora*	Leaves—salad, cooked greens.
Mountain Ash	*Sorbus* (sp)	Fruit—jelly, hot tea.
Mustard (Wild, Summer)	*Brassica* (sp)	Leaves—salad, cooked greens.
Paw Paw	*Asimina triloba*	Fruit—raw after being frostbitten.
Pecans	*Carya illinoensis*	Nut meats—raw, toasted, in baking, etc.
Persimmon	*Diospyros virginiana*	Fruit—raw after being frostbitten.
Piñon Nuts	*Pinus cembroides*	Seed in cones—raw, toasted, ground as flour.
Plantain (Common)	*Plantaco major*	Young leaves—cooked greens.
Pokeweed	*Phytolacca decandra*	Young shoots (under 4 in.)—like asparagus (two waters).
Plums	*Prunus* (sp)	Fruit—raw, sauce, jam, etc.
Purslane (Pussley)	*Portulaca oleracea*	Leaf and stems—salad, cooked greens.

165

Plant	Botanical Name	Edible Parts & Uses
Raspberry	*Rubus* (sp)	Berries—raw, jam, etc.
Red Mulberry	*Morus* (sp)	Berries—raw, pies, preserves.
Sassafras	*Sassafras variifolium*	Buds, leaves, flowers—steeped for hot tea. Root bark boiled for hot tea.
Spearmint	*Mentha spicata*	Leaves — flavoring for vegetables, etc., steeped for hot or cold tea.
Staghorn Sumac (Smooth, Mountain)	*Rhus* (sp)	Berries—steeped for pink 'lemonade.'
Strawberries	*Fragaria* (sp)	Berries—raw, jams, etc. Leaves—hot tea.
Water Chinquapin	*Nelumbo lutea*	Seeds—raw, toasted.
Water Cress	*Radicula nasturtium-aquaticum*	Leaves, tender shoots—salad, cooked greens.
Wild Rice	*Zizania aquatica*	Seeds—dried, boiled like white rice.
Wintergreen	*Gaultheria procumbens*	Fruit, raw leaves—flavoring.

APPENDIX

HELPFUL HINTS AND REMINDERS

1. To simplify dishwashing, rub coating of soap or other detergent on outside of utensils before placing over the fire.
2. Use sand, wood ashes, or grasses to scour kettles.
3. Hang kettle over fire before lighting to get every bit of heat.
4. Cook over embers (glowing coals) for steady even heat. Flames are quick and hot, but smoky.
5. To banish fish odor from pots and pans, boil a little water and vinegar in them.
6. Grease the inside of a pan before melting chocolate in it.
7. Grease the inside of a cup before measuring molasses in it.
8. Wrap a bottle or pail in a well-soaked cloth or paper and hang it in a breeze in the shade to keep it cool.
9. Make use of bacon drippings to save on carrying other fats or shortening. Vegetable fats do not burn or smoke as easily as butter or lard.
10. Measure flour before carrying to camp site to save on equipment.
11. Test eggs in the shell for freshness. Old doubtful ones float on the top of a pan of cold water; fresh ones sink.
12. Carry margarine or canned butter when refrigeration or cooling for fresh butter is not available. Keep butter fresh in steril-

ized, tightly closed jars. Store in a spring, weighted or secured in safe cold running water or wrapped in wet cloths (See number 8).

13. Substitute for baking powder: equal amounts of the *white* of wood ashes mixed with flour. Ash makes hot breads rise just as soda does. Ashes from hickory, dogwood, and sugar maple are best. Also useful are ashes from beech, ash, buckeye, and poplar woods.

14. Stand sandwich on edge (not laid flat), in sack (nosebag) or box lunch to prevent sogginess of bread slices.

15. Carry an orange, peach, or other juicy fruit on the trail to quench thirst and for a quick pickup.

16. One pound of the dried fruit is equal to six pounds of apples, three pounds of peaches, or two pounds of plums.

17. Bitter sweet (semi-sweet) chocolate will not make you as thirsty as sweet milk chocolate.

18. Processed cheeses in unopened containers require no refrigeration.

19. Tubes of margarine or butter, jam, mustard, catsup, and condensed milk are compact and light weight for trail packing.

20. Try out recipes in your home kitchen or backyard to test the quantities, procedures, number of servings, and needed equipment before going off on a canoe trip or weekend, etc.

21. Know the conservation laws and rules of the locality before cutting toasting sticks, building fires, or picking flowers.

22. Choose your fire type and fuel to suit your menu and equipment.

23. Have plenty of a few (3 to 4) different foods rather than small amounts of many things.

24. Keep raw vegetables crisp by washing at

home and wrapping in damp cloth, wax paper, or plastic bag.

25. Pick high protein, high calorie foods for maximum food values and minimum weight when backpacking.

26. Include dried and dehydrated fruit and vegetables when backpacking for necessary vitamins, minerals, and bulk.

27. Use hard woods to make a bed of embers (glowing coals) or soft resinous wood for quick, hot flames, but with no embers later.

28. Have bed of coals only 2 to 3 in. deep.

29. Keep your knives sharp for safety and also to cut more easily.

30. *Always* take along a first-aid kit.

31. Leave the camp site in even better condition than you found it. Be sure the fire is out cold (Chapter 5).

32. Sanitize eating dishes, especially cups, glasses, spoons, and forks by scalding in boiling water (at least 170° to 180° F.) for two minutes.

33. Pour cereal slowly into salted boiling water and keep the water boiling to prevent lumps in hot cereals.

34. Put fire out quickly with less water by sprinkling, not pouring water on coals or embers.

35. You need almost as much equipment for a weekend of outdoor cooking as for two weeks of it.

36. Know the poisonous plants of the area and avoid them.

37. Reseal opened evaporated milk cans with scotch tape or adhesive tape over the punctured holes.

	SUNDAY	MONDAY	TUESDAY

BREAKFAST	½ grapefruit
	Nalasniki
	  (Polish pancake)
	bacon
	cocoa or milk
		stewed prunes
		scrambled eggs
		biscuits
		jam
		cocoa or milk
			orange
			cereal with dates
			Sally Lunn muffins
			  and jam
			cocoa or milk

LUNCH	ham (or beef stew),
	sweet potatoes and
	  orange casserole
	string beans
	prune whip
	chocolate milk
		volcano potatoes
		fresh tomatoes
		bread & butter
		mock angel food cake
		milk
			baked eggs in orange
			  hulls
			peanut butter and
			  raisin sandwich
			banana boats
			milk

SUPPER	cream of pea soup
	fruit salad
	crackers; bread and
	  butter
	cookies and
	  milk
		savory sausage
		  and spaghetti
		tossed salad
		bread and butter
		apple crisp
		milk
			Spanish rice
			shredded cabbage
			apple and nut salad
			short cut fudge
			milk

Substitutions may easily be made in these menus for regional or religious reasons.
Plan to use seasonal and local fruits and vegetables to cut down on costs.

ONE-WEEK CAMP
persons

WEDNESDAY	THURSDAY	FRIDAY	SATURDAY

applesauce
broiled ham (or eggs)
toast and marmalade
cocoa or milk
	tomato juice
	ready-to-serve cereal
	creamed chipped beef
	  on toast
	cocoa or milk
		stewed apricots
		French toast with
		  honey and butter
		cocoa or milk
			stewed mixed fruits
			pancakes
			apple butter
			cocoa or milk

corn chowder
pilot crackers
bread & butter
cole slaw
fruit balls
milk
	scrambled eggs (with
	  crisp bacon)
	baked potato
	celery sticks with
	  peanut butter
	bread and jam
	milk
		chicken soup with
		  noodles
		asparagus and
		  egg salad
		bread, butter
		  and jelly
		apple somemores
		milk
			Hopping John
			apple cheese salad
			bread twist with jam
			milk

green peppers stuffed
  with ground meat
  & tomato sauce
carrot sticks
Hawaiian Island
milk
	baked bean hole beans
	brown bread
	pear and
	  watercress salad
	cake with hot fudge
	  sauce
	milk
		macaroni and cheese
		peas with pimento
		sliced tomatoes
		bread and butter
		fruit cup
		milk
			creamed tuna on toast
			buttered carrots
			orange date salad
			blackberry roll
			milk

SUPPLIES FOR A ONE-WEEK CAMP

Staple order for a 1-week period or 21 meals for 12.

These quantities have been set up for an easily divisible number so they can be increased or decreased as the number of campers require. Peanut butter is listed for snacks and as a meal supplement; it is not included in the menus.

1. Beverages

2 lbs. cocoa
½ lb. unsweetened chocolate

2. Cereals

1 lb. pkg. uncooked cereal
1 ready-to-serve cereal (13 oz.) or 12 individual pkgs.

3. Soups (Canned)

4 (10 oz.) cans cream of pea soup
2 (10 oz.) cans tomato soup
4 (10 oz.) cans cream pea soup soups (dehydrated)
6 oz. jar of chicken soup base

4. Dairy Products and Meats

5 lbs. bacon
1½ lbs. salt fat pork
4 lbs. American Cheese
1 lb. cottage cheese
6 lbs. ham
4 tall (15 oz.) cans condensed milk
6 (14½ oz.) cans evaporated milk (for cooking).
2 lb. jar or can of peanut butter

5. Fish

3 cans (13 oz.) tuna fish (or 2 cans salmon)

6. Vegetables

5 lbs. sweet potatoes
15 lbs. white potatoes
3 lbs. onions
2 lbs. dried black-eyed peas
3 lbs. dried navy beans
3 (1 lb. 4 oz.) cans corn
2 qts. tomatoes
4 (1 lb.) cans spaghetti with cheese and tomato sauce
3 (1 lb. 4 oz.) cans asparagus
3 (1 lb. 4 oz.) cans peas
1 (8 oz.) can pimento

7. Flour and Bread

12 lbs. flour
½ lb. noodles
1 lb. macaroni
3 loaves Boston
Brown bread

8. Condiments

1 box salt
1 box pepper
1 can baking powder
1 small box mustard
1 small box cinnamon
1 small box nutmeg
1 small box paprika
1 small bottle vanilla
1 qt. vinegar
1 bottle catsup (14 oz.)
1 qt. mayonnaise
2 bottles (1 pt.)
French dressing
2 lbs. vegetable
shortening

9. Fruit (Canned)

2 (1 lb. 13 oz.) cans
applesauce
3 (9 oz.) cans sliced
pineapple
3 (1 lb. 13 oz.) cans
pears
2 (1 lb. 4 oz.) cans
blackberries (if
fresh berries are
not available)

10. Fruit (Dried) and Nuts

4 lbs. prunes
3 lbs. apricots
3 lbs. raisins
3 lbs. dates
3 lbs. peaches
1 lb. figs
3 lbs. nuts (shelled)
2 lbs. peanuts
(salted)

11. Cookies and Crackers

2 pkgs. pilot
crackers
3 pkgs. saltines
(1 lb. each)
2 lbs. mixed sweet
cookies

12. Sugar and Sweets

8 lbs. sugar
3 lbs. brown sugar
1 qt. jam
1 pt. apple butter
1 pt. honey
1 pt. jelly
1 pt. marmalade
1 lb. marshmallows

	SUNDAY	MONDAY	TUESDAY
BREAKFAST	6 grapefruit 5 eggs ½ lb. butter* 4 qts. milk	12 eggs ½ lb. butter 4 qts. milk	12 oranges ½ lb. butter 3 eggs 4 qts. milk
LUNCH	4 oranges 3 lbs. string beans 4 qts. milk	½ lb. butter 4 lbs. tomatoes 2 loaves unsliced bread 2 loaves sliced bread 4 qts. milk	12 eggs 4 loaves bread 12 bananas 4 qts. milk
SUPPER	10 oranges 3 grapefruit 1 lb. grapes 2 heads lettuce 4 qts. milk 2 loaves sliced bread ¼ lb. butter	24 link sausages 2 cucumbers 2 heads lettuce 1 lb. spinach 1 bunch carrots ½ lb. butter 12 apples 4 qts. milk	2 cabbages ¼ lb. butter 12 apples 4 qts. milk

*Use butter or margarine throughout the week. Save and use bacon drippings.

ONE-WEEK CAMP
to staple order)
servings for twelve persons

WEDNESDAY	THURSDAY	FRIDAY	SATURDAY
½ lb. butter 3 loaves bread 4 qts. milk	2 lbs. chipped beef 3 loaves bread 5 qts. milk	3 loaves bread ½ lb. butter 6 eggs 4 qts. milk	4 eggs ½ lb. butter 4 qts. milk
2 cabbages 5 qts. milk 2 loaves sliced bread ¼ lb. butter	12 eggs 2 bunches celery ½ lb. butter 3 loaves bread 4 qts. milk	6 eggs 2 heads lettuce 12 apples ½ lb. butter 3 loaves bread 4 qts. milk	8 apples ½ lb. butter 4 qts. milk
12 green peppers 3 lbs. ground steak 3 bunches carrots 2 loaves bread ½ lb. butter 3 qts. milk	2 bunches watercress 2 pound cakes 4 qts. milk	4 lbs. tomatoes 10 oranges 6 apples 4 qts. milk	3 loaves bread 3 bunches carrots ¼ lb. butter 10 oranges 2 heads lettuce 5 qts. milk

EQUIPMENT FOR A ONE-WEEK CAMP

This equipment is recommended as adequate for a troop camp for 12 persons who are using the type of menus suggested in this book.

Cooking Equipment

1 (9¼ qt.) kettle
  and
1 (6¾ qt.) kettle
  or
1 set of nested pots*
1 water bucket (2 gal.)
2 frying pans
2 milk pails or
  covered pails
  (6½ qts.)
2 folding reflector
  ovens*
2 muffin pans
  (12-hole)

1 measuring cup
  (1 pt.)
1 set measuring
  spoons
2 tin plates
1 set salt and pepper
  shakers
1 long-handled fork*
1 long-handled
  spoon*
1 paring knife
1 large knife
1 pair utility tongs
1 large Dutch oven*

2 deep pans for
  baking (2½"x12")
3 mixing bowls
  (large, medium,
  small)
2 rolls heavy
  aluminum foil

1 can opener
  (jackknife* or
  regular one if
  room to carry)
containers for
  staples

Dining Equipment

It is recommended that dishes and service equipment for the troop camp be of unbreakable ware, such as metal or plastic which is like lightweight. Plastic must stand the 180°—212° F. water used in sanitizing.

16 plates*
16 cups*
16 cereal or dessert
  bowls*
14 knives*
14 spoons*
14 forks*
  2 service spoons*

1 large platter*
2—4 qt. pitchers
2 vegetable serving
  dishes*
1 creamer
1 sugar bowl
2 pairs salt and
  pepper shakers

*Items marked with an asterisk are available from your Girl Scout Agency or National Equipment Service.

Dishwashing Equipment and Housekeeping Supplies

2 galvanized tubs
  (16 qts.)
1 wire rack*
  (leave dish towels
  at home)
1 package matches
  (waterproofed)
2 large boxes soap
  or syndet (or
  liquid detergent)

2 cakes yellow soap
2 mops or dishcloths
2 yards cheesecloth
1 package steel wool
500 paper napkins
4 rolls paper towels
  (use to dry pots if
  necessary to
  prevent rusting)

Miscellaneous

2 packbaskets*
1 rucksack*
1 ax*
2 pairs work gloves
1 hatchet*

1 shovel* (rapid
  digger)
1 waterbag (2 gal.
  waterproof canvas)
first-aid kit*

*Items marked with an asterisk are available from your Girl Scout Agency or National Equipment Service.

FOOD FOR BACKPACKING

Menus for backpacking trips require thoughtful planning. They must be nutritious, simple, substantial, light in weight, and pre-tested at home. They should be easily prepared on the trail with minimum equipment. Dehydrated foods and those of high caloric value cut down on bulk and weight and can be combined to meet the daily food requirements of hikers.

There are many types of dehydrated foods. Look for such items as dehydrated beets, carrots, spinach, cabbage, onions, tomatoes, parsley flakes, soups, dry milk, and powdered eggs on the shelves of local grocery stores. In addition, you will find that sporting goods stores, outdoor equipment outfitters, and food supply houses carry a variety of trail foods. Some also feature completely packaged dehydrated trail meals.

It is most important to pretest dehydrated

177

foods. For example, most of them require only 2/3 the amount of water specified on the package. All are improved with seasonings. Experiment at home, and use imagination. Be alert for new items such as dehydrated applesauce with sugar. Try combinations. For example, have you thought of mixing dry eggs, salt, nutmeg, dry milk, dry vanilla, and lemon powder? The result will be a fine trail egg nog. Rice and cheese dishes provide a maximum of calories and proteins and are universally popular. Other suggestions are listed below.

Again, it is necessary to reiterate the importance of knowing your route and its facilities before planning menus. All dehydrates require considerable water. Will safe, tested water be easy to secure along the trail? You may discover that dehydrated food is more trouble than it is worth. Buying along the way should be investigated. On some trails, stores are near the trail.

High protein foods include: dried beans, egg noodles, oatmeal, soy flour, all cheeses, dry skim milk, peanuts, peanut butter, dried beef, most canned meats, dried whole eggs, canned tuna. Because the protein requirement is most difficult to meet, it is wise to select those foods first and then complete the menu with high calorie foods. It is always necessary to include dried or dehydrated fruits and vegetables. They provide vitamins, minerals, and bulk in the diet.

When planning menus, remember that you get the maximum nourishment by choosing foods with the most calories per ounce.

At least 100 calories per ounce

Cornmeal	Butter or margarine
Macaroni products	Cheese
Oatmeal	Dry skim milk
Rice	Peanuts and peanut butter
Whole wheat flour	Bacon
Instant potato	Dried whole eggs

At least 90 calories per ounce

Dried tomato, onions, carrots, cabbage

At least 80 to 90 calories per ounce

Dried apples, apricots, dates, figs, peaches, prunes, raisins

Experiment by adding other foods to the dehydrated or high calorie foods. For example, try:

1. Dried beef with macaroni or spaghetti.
2. Tomato and onion flakes with spaghetti.
3. Onion flakes with potato.
4. Dried beef or cheese with rice or potato.
5. Crisp bacon or vinegar with cabbage.
6. Cabbage soaked for ½ hour and eaten raw as cole slaw.
7. Gingerbread dumplings with applesauce.
8. Bacon or bacon fat with vegetables (easier to carry them).

9. Dehydrated syrup on hot cereal.
10. Raisins or dates with hot cereal or rice.
11. Rice or cornmeal as a morning cereal.
12. Dried apricots with peaches.
13. Raisins with dried apricots.
14. Small amount of lemon with prunes or dried apples.
15. Dried fruit compote (apples, peaches, apricots, prunes).

A High Calorie, High Protein Lunch Suggestion

6 or 8 triscuits
2 or 3 oz. cheese
6 prunes or a handful of raisins
1 bar bitter-sweet chocolate or hard candy
  (easier to carry, lasts longer)
1 carrot
1 orange (if weight permits)

179

List of Foods and Staples with Equivalents for Weight and Measure

Apples, chopped ....   1 lb. ....   3 C.
Apricots, dried ......   1 lb. ....   3 C.
    cooked, drained..   1 lb. ....   5 C.
Baking powder ....   6 oz. ....   1 C.
                  1 oz. ....2⅔ Tbsp.
Baking soda ....   1 oz. ....2½ Tbsp.
Beans, dried ....   1 lb. ....2½ C.
Beans, dried ....2½ C. .... 6½ C. (cooked)
Bread crumbs, dry ..   1 lb. ....   5 C.
Butter ....   1 lb. ....   2 C.
   1 stick ....   ¼ lb. ....   8 Tbsp.
Chocolate ....   1 lb. .... 16 sq.
Cocoa ....   1 lb. ....   4 C.
Cornmeal ....   1 lb. ....   3 C. (12 C. cooked)
Cornstarch ....   1 lb. ....   3 C.
                  1 oz. ....   4 Tbsp.
Cream ....   1 qt. ....   doubles when whipped

Dates ....   1 lb. ....   2 C. chopped
Eggs, whole   5   ....   1 C.
Eggs, whites 8-9   ....   1 C.
Eggs, yolks   12   ....   1 C.
Flour ....   1 lb. ....   4 C.
Macaroni, before
   cooking ....   1 lb. ....   4 C.
                      (9 C. cooked)
Molasses ....   12 oz. ....   1 C.
Noodles, before
   cooking ....   1 lb. ....   6 C.
                      (9 C. cooked)
Onions ....   1 lb. .... 2-3 C.
Peanut butter ....   1 lb. ....   2 C.
Potatoes ....   1 bu. .... 60 lbs.
Potato chips ....   1 lb. ....   5 qts.
Raisins, seeded ......   1 lb. ....3¼ C.
Raisins, seedless ....   1 lb. ....2¾ C.
Rice, before cooking   1 lb. ....   2 C.
Rice, after cooking..   1 lb. ....   2 qts.
Spaghetti, after
   cooking ....   1 lb. ....2½ qts.
Sugar, brown ....   1 lb. ....2¼ C.

Sugar, granulated ..	1 lb.	2 C.
Sugar, powdered	1 lb. ....3½ C.	
Tea	1 lb. ....6½ C. (300 servings)	
Vanilla	1 oz.....	2 Tbsp.
Coffee (ground)	1 lb.	5 C. (40-50 servings)
Mustard	1 oz.....	5 Tbsp.
Salt	1 oz.....1½ Tbsp.	

Fresh Vegetables—Servings Per Pound

vegetable	how prepared	approx. servings per pound
Beans (yellow or green)	Buttered (in pieces)	4-5
Beans	Creamed	5-6
Beets	Buttered	4
Cabbage	Buttered	3-4
Carrots	Buttered (diced)	3
Carrots	Creamed	3-4
Cauliflower	Buttered	3
Onions	Buttered	4
Potatoes	Whole (medium)	3
Spinach	Buttered	3-4
Swiss chard	Buttered	4
Squash, summer	Mashed or diced	3-4

181

WEIGHTS AND MEASUREMENTS
Abbreviations

t or tsp.	teaspoon
T or Tbsp.	tablespoon
C.	cup
# or lb.	pound
pt.	pint
qt.	quart
gal.	gallon
No. or #	number
bu.	bushel
pk.	peck
sq.	square
oz.	ounce

Campers' Measurements Without Utensils

1 open fistful	½ C.
five-finger pinch	1 Tbsp.
four-finger pinch	1 tsp.
one-finger pinch (with thumb)	⅛ tsp.
one-finger gob of shortening	1 Tbsp.
palm of hand (center)	1 Tbsp.

Equivalents

1 Tbsp.	3 tsp.
1 qt.	4 cups
1 fluid qt.	32 oz.
1 C.	16 Tbsp. (8 oz.)
1 pk.	8 qts.
1 bu.	4 pks.
1 lb.	16 oz.
No. 303 can	2 C.
No. 2 can	2½ C. or 20 oz.
No. 2½ can	3½ C. or 29 oz.
No. 10 can	13 C. or 6½ lbs.

Evaporated Milk

Thoroughly mix evaporated milk and water and use it as fluid milk. One pt. evaporated milk plus 1 pt. water makes 1 qt. fluid milk. One small can evaporated milk contains ⅔ cups. One tall can evaporated milk (14½ oz.) contains 1⅔ cups.

Dried Milk

Follow manufacturer's directions. Use dry with other dry ingredients. Reconstitute (approx. 1 cup dried milk in 1 qt. water equals approx. 1 qt. fluid milk.)

Dried Eggs

Sprinkle dried egg over surface of water or use with other dry ingredients. Use equal parts dried egg and water (2½ Tbsp. dried egg plus 2½ Tbsp. water equals 1 whole egg).

Substitutions

1 C. molasses	1 C. honey
1⅛ C. brown sugar	½ lb. brown sugar
1¾ C. powdered sugar	½ lb. powdered sugar
1 oz. chocolate (1 sq.)..	3 Tbsp. cocoa plus 1 Tbsp. fat
1 C. honey	1 to 1¼ C. sugar plus ¼ C. liquid
1 Tbsp. flour	½ Tbsp. cornstarch for thickening

BIBLIOGRAPHY

GIRL SCOUT RESOURCES

The following publications may be ordered from Girl Scout National Equipment Service, 830 Third Avenue, New York, N.Y. 10022.

Feeding a Crowd, Cat. No. 19-977
Firebuilding, Cat. No. 26-212
Happily Appley—A Leader's Guide to Food Fun with Young Children. Cat. No. 19-995
Primitive Camp Sanitation, Cat. No. 26-215
Safety-Wise, Cat. No. 26-205
Toolcraft, Cat. No. 26-214
Worlds to Explore: Handbook for Brownie and Junior Girl Scouts, Cat. No. 20-700

For a complete list of available resources, write for a free Publications /Audiovisual Catalog.

OTHER RESOURCES

Better Homes and Gardens New Junior Cook Book. Des Moines, Iowa: Meredith Corporation, 1979

Camping and Woodcraft, H. Kephart. New York: Macmillan, 1948

Food for Knapsackers and Other Trail Travelers, H. Bunnelle. San Francisco: Sierra Club Books, 1971

Garden Spice and Wild-Pot Herbs, W. C. Muenscher and M. A. Rice. Ithaca, New York: Cornell University Press, paperback 1978

Roughing It Easy, D. Thomas. New York: Warner Books, 1974

United Nations Cookbook, Barbara Kraus. New York: Simon & Schuster, Inc., 1970

Wildwood Wisdom, E. Jaeger. New York: Macmillan, 1966

Your Own Book of Campcraft, Catherine T. Hammett. New York: Pocket Books, Inc., paperback 1971

Sources for Organizational Publications

American Home Economics Association, 2010 Massachusetts Avenue, N. W., Washington, D.C. 20036

Appalachian Trail Conference, P.O. Box 236, Harpers Ferry, W. Va. 25425

Boy Scouts of America, P.O. Box 61030, Dallas/ Fort Worth Airport Station, Dallas, Tex. 75261

Camp Fire Inc., 4601 Madison Avenue, Kansas City, Mo. 64112

Sierra Club Books, 530 Bush Street, San Francisco, Calif. 94108

Sources for Government Publications

Federal: Superintendent of Documents, Government Printing Office, Washington, D.C. 20402 (for inexpensive publications on dried eggs, dried milk, campfire cooking, school lunch program, food plants, etc., from the U.S. Department of Agriculture; other pamphlets on emergency mass feeding, on public health practices, etc.)

State: Write to your own State or County Extension Service or to the land-grant college or university in your state.

Sources of Business-Sponsored Publications on Outdoor Cooking

American Dry Milk Institute, Inc., 130 North Franklin Street, Chicago, Ill. 60606

Ann Pillsbury, The Pillsbury Company, 608 Second Avenue S., Minneapolis, Minn. 55402

Campbell Soup Company, Campbell Place, Camden, N.J. 08101

Evaporated Milk Association, 15 West Montgomery Avenue, Rockville, Md. 20850

General Foods Corporation, 250 North Street, White Plains, N.Y. 10625

General Mills, Inc., 9200 Wayzata Boulevard, Minneapolis, Minn. 55440

Kaiser Aluminum & Chemical Corp., 300 Lakeside Drive, Oakland, Calif. 94643

Home Economics Services, Kellogg Company, Battle Creek, Mich. 49016

National Dairy Council, 6300 North River Road, Rosemont, Ill. 60018

The Nestlé Company, Inc., 100 Bloomingdale Road, White Plains, N.Y. 10605

Ocean Spray Cranberries, Inc., Plymouth, Mass. 02360

Reynolds Metals Company, 6601 Broad Street Road, Richmond, Va. 23261

Stokely-Van Camp, Inc., 941 North Meridian Street, Indianapolis, Ind. 46206

RECIPE INDEX

Recipes—Serve 12	Page Ref.	Menu Item	Main Ingred.	Ease of Prep.*	Total Prep. Time†	Origin
American Goulash	62	main	beef, spaghetti	E		
Angels on Horseback	87	main	cheese, bacon	E	½ hr.	
Apple Charlotte	122	dessert	apple, bread oranges	E		
Apple Cobbler	119	dessert	apple, biscuit mix	B		
Apfel Pfannkuchen	72	breakfast, dessert	flour, apples	E	½ hr.	Germany
Apple Crisp	121	dessert	flour, apples	B		
Apple Delight	146	dessert	apples, biscuit mix	E		
Apple Cheese and Watercress	36	salad	cheese, apples, watercress	B	½ hr.	
Applesauce Pancake	73	breakfast, dessert	flour, applesauce, eggs	E	½ hr.	
Arroz con Pollo	61	main	chicken, rice, vegetables	A	2 hrs.	Cuba, Mexico
Asparagus Alternates	159	vegetable	wild fern	A		
Asparagus and Egg	36	salad	eggs, asparagus	B	½ hr.	

187

* Beginner (B); Experienced (E); Advanced (A).
† Includes fire-building time; ½ hr. or less (½ hr.); 2 hr. or more (2 hr.). Where time is not indicated, preparation takes between ½ hr. and 2 hr.

Recipes—Serve 12	Page Ref.	Menu Item	Main Ingred.	Ease of Prep.*	Total Prep. Time†	Origin
Bacon an' Egg on a Rock	152	breakfast	bacon, eggs	E	½ hr.	
Bacon-Banana-on-a-Stick	88	main	bananas, bacon	E	½ hr.	
Bags of Gold	70	main	flour, cheese	E		
Baked Apple	120	dessert	apples, coconut	E		
Baked Apple (embers)	140	dessert	apples	E		
Baked Apple (foil)	146	dessert	apples	E	½ hr.	
Baked Apple with Banana	120	dessert	bananas, apples	E		
Baked Avocado	109	vegetable	avocados, bread crumbs	E		S.E. U.S.
Baked Banana	147	dessert	bananas	E		
Baked Eggs in the Shell	142	breakfast	eggs	E		
Baked Frankfurters	107	main	frankfurters, spices sauce	E		
Banana and Mint	39	salad	bananas, mint	B	½ hr.	
Banana Boats	142	dessert	bananas, marsh-mallows, chocolate	E		
Banana Boats (foil)	147	dessert	bananas	E		
Banana Fritters with Orange Sauce	72	bread, dessert	flour, eggs, bananas, oranges	A		
Banana Nut Pancakes with Lemon Sauce	73	breakfast, dessert	mix, bananas, nut-meats, lemon	B	½ hr.	

188

* Beginner (B); Experienced (E); Advanced (A).
† Includes fire-building time; ½ hr. or less (½ hr.); 2 hr. or more (2 hr.). Where time is not indicated, preparation takes between ½ hr. and 2 hr.

Recipes—Serve 12	Page Ref.	Menu Item	Main Ingred.	Ease of Prep.*	Total Prep. Time†	Origin
Banana Whip	40	dessert	bananas, lemon	B	½ hr.	
Barbecued Chicken— Method 1	93	main	roasting chicken (whole), sauce	A	2 hrs.	
Barbecued Chicken— Method 2	94	main	broilers (split), sauce	A	2 hrs.	
Barbecued Chops or Beef	94	main	lamb, beef, pork	E	½ hr.	
Barbecued Pork	94	main	pork	A	2 hrs.	
Barbecue Sauce (for poultry)	95	sauce	oil, vinegar	E		
Barbecue Sauce (Pineapple— for meat)	95	sauce	brown sugar, vinegar, pineapple juice	E		
Barbecue Sauce (Teriyaki— for meat)	95	sauce	pineapple, soy sauce, ginger	E		
Barbecued Turkey or Duck	94	meat	poultry, sauce	A	2 hrs.	
Bean Hole Beans	130	main	beans, salt pork, molasses	A	2 hrs.	
Beef Stew	144	main	beef, bacon, tomatoes	E	2 hrs.	
Beet Borsch	52	soup	beets, milk	E		Russia
Birchermuesli	40	dessert	oatmeal flakes, milk, fruits	B	2 hrs.	Switzerland
Bird's Nest	34	salad	tomatoes, cheese	B	½ hr.	
Biscuits	112	bread	flour, shortening	E	½ hr.	

* Beginner (B); Experienced (E); Advanced (A).
† Includes fire-building time; ½ hr. or less (½ hr.); 2 hr. or more (2 hr.). Where time is not indicated, preparation takes between ½ hr. and 2 hr.

Recipes—Serve 12	Page Ref.	Menu Item	Main Ingred.	Ease of Prep.*	Total Prep. Time†	Origin
Biscuits	113, 146	bread	mix	E	½ hr.	
Biscuit Mix	113	bread	flour	B	½ hr.	
Blueberry Muffins	115	bread	flour, blueberries	E	½ hr.	
Blushing Bunny	65	main	soup, cheese, flour	B	½ hr.	
Bran Muffins	114	bread	flour, bran, eggs	E		
Bread Griddle Cakes	47	breakfast, bread	eggs, bread crumbs	B	½ hr.	
Bread Twisters or Doughboys	87	bread	flour, shortening, biscuit mix	E	½ hr.	
Breakfast Egg	154	breakfast	eggs, bacon	E	½ hr.	
Bunny	35	salad	lettuce, cheese	B	½ hr.	
Butterscotch Sauce	76	dessert	brown sugar, corn-starch	E	½ hr.	
Cake	146	dessert	mix	E		
Cake Toppings	117	dessert	various	B	½ hr.	
California Egg Crackle	51	breakfast, main	bacon, eggs	B	½ hr.	
Campfire Stew	60	main	beef, soup	B	½ hr.	
Candied Apples	77	dessert	corn sirup, apples	E		
Carrot and Apple	37	salad	apple, carrot	B	½ hr.	
Celery Sticks	35	salad	celery, cheese	B	½ hr.	

* Beginner (B); Experienced (E); Advanced (A).
† Includes fire-building time; ½ hr. or less (½ hr.); 2 hr. or more (2 hr.). Where time is not indicated, preparation takes between ½ hr. and 2 hr.

Recipes—Serve 12	Page Ref.	Menu Item	Main Ingred.	Ease of Prep.*	Total Prep. Time†	Origin
Cereals	48	breakfast	oatmeal, wheat, corn	B	½ hr.	
Cheese Balls and Watercress	35	salad	cottage cheese, nuts, watercress	B	½ hr.	
Cheese Biscuits	114	bread	flour, cheese	E	½ hr.	
Cheese Toast	112	bread, main	bread, cheese	B	½ hr.	
Cherry Delight	118	dessert	pie filling, flour	E		
Chicken and Dumplings	139	main	chickens, vegetables	E		
Chicken Imu	132	main	chickens, vegetables	A	2 hrs.	
Chili Con Carne	57	main	chili, beef, beans	B	½ hr.	Mexico
Chocolate (Hot)	82	beverage	chocolate, milk	B	½ hr.	
Chocolate Popcorn	78	candy	chocolate, popcorn	B		
Chocolate Sauce	76	dessert	cornstarch, cocoa	E	½ hr.	
Circled Eggs	152	breakfast	eggs	E	½ hr.	
Clam Bake	131	main	clams, corn, sea-weed	A	2 hrs.	
Cobblers	117, 119, 147	dessert	fruit, biscuit mix	B		
Cocoa	82	beverage	cocoa, milk	B	½ hr.	
Cocoa Fudge	77	candy	cocoa, corn sirup	E	½ hr.	
Coconut Cream Candy	77	candy	coconut, sugar	E	½ hr.	S.E.U.S.

* Beginner (B); Experienced (E); Advanced (A).
† Includes fire-building time; ½ hr. or less (½ hr.); 2 hr. or more (2 hr.). Where time is not indicated, preparation takes between ½ hr. and 2 hr.

Recipes—Serve 12	Page Ref.	Menu Item	Main Ingred.	Ease of Prep.*	Total Prep. Time†	Origin
Cocoroons	119	dessert	eggs, corn flakes, coconut	B		
Coffee Cake	117	bread, dessert	biscuit mix, fruit	E		
Coffee Can Stew	138	main	bacon, beef, vegetable	E		
Cole Slaw	38	salad	cabbage, pineapple, raisins	B	½ hr.	
Cooked Greens	159	vegetable	wild greens	A		
Corn Bread	110	bread	cornmeal	E		
Corn Chowder	54	main	bacon, potatoes, corn	E		
Corn Flake Chews	78	candy	corn flakes, brown sugar	E	½ hr.	
Corn on the Cob	95	vegetable	corn in husks	E	½ hr.	
Corn on the Cob (foil)	144	vegetable	ears of corn	E	½ hr.	
Corn Oysters	69	vegetable	corn, flour	A		
Corn Roast	127	vegetable	corn in husks	E		
Corn Yum-Yum	70	main	bacon, eggs, corn	B		
Cottage Cheese Combinations	34	salad	cottage cheese	B	½ hr.	
Cranberry Applesauce	75	dessert	apples, cranberries	B	½ hr.	
Creamed Chipped Beef	58	main	milk, beef, potatoes	E		

*Beginner (B); Experienced (E); Advanced (A).
†Includes fire-building time; ½ hr. or less (½ hr.); 2 hr. or more (2 hr.). Where time is not indicated, preparation takes between ½ hr. and 2 hr.

Recipes—Serve 12	Page Ref.	Menu Item	Main Ingred.	Ease of Prep.*	Total Prep. Time†	Origin
Creamed Eggs	51	main	flour, eggs	B	½ hr.	
Date Loaf Candy	81	candy	dates, pecans	E		
Desert Fish	56	main	pork, milk	E	½ hr.	S.W. U.S.
Double Boiler Bread	50	bread	cornmeal, caraway seeds	A		
Doughnut Delights	97	dessert	doughnuts, jelly	B	½ hr.	
Dried Fruit	42	dessert, salad	dried fruits, nut-meats	B	2 hrs.	
Dried Milk for Drinking	42	beverage	powdered milk	B	½ hr.	
Eggs in a Hole	153	breakfast, egg	bacon, eggs, bread	E		
Eggs in Tomato Cups	103	main	tomatoes, eggs, cheese	E		
Egg Nog	43	beverage	milk, eggs	B	½ hr.	
Eggs on a Stick	155	breakfast, main	eggs	A	½ hr.	
Elderflower Pancakes	160	bread	flour, elderflower	A		
Evaporated Milk for Drinking	43	beverage	evaporated milk	B	½ hr.	
Faar i Kaal	59	main	lamb, cabbage	E	2 hrs.	Norway

193

* Beginner (B); Experienced (E); Advanced (A).
† Includes fire-building time; ½ hr. or less (½ hr.); 2 hr. or more (2 hr.). Where time is not indicated, preparation takes between ½ hr. and 2 hr.

Recipes—Serve 12	Page Ref.	Menu Item	Main Ingred.	Ease of Prep.*	Total Prep. Time†	Origin
Fairy Rings	97	dessert	doughnuts, marsh-mallows	B	½ hr.	
Fillet of Fish	143	main	fish	E	½ hr.	
Flapjacks	47	bread	flour, eggs	E	½ hr.	
Frankfurters	91	main	frankfurters	E	½ hr.	
Frankfurter Kabobs	90	main	frankfurter, vegetable	E		
French Dressing	38	salad	lemon, honey, oil	B	½ hr.	
French Onion Soup	53	soup	onions, cheese	E	2 hrs.	France
French Toast	48	breakfast, main	eggs, bread	B	½ hr.	
Fried Tomatoes and Eggs in Cream Sauce	66	main	tomatoes, eggs	E		
Frozen Graham Cracker Pudding	41	dessert	evaporated milk, graham cracker crumbs	A	2 hrs.	
Fruit Balls	40	candy	dried fruits, honey	B	½ hr.	
Fruit Milk Shake	44	beverage	juice, milk	B	½ hr.	
Fruit Punch—Powdered	44	beverage	fruit flavors	B	½ hr.	
Fruits and Nuts	160	dessert	wild foods	A		
Frukt Suppe	54	soup, dessert	prunes, spices	B		Norway

*Beginner (B); Experienced (E); Advanced (A).
†Includes fire-building time; ½ hr. or less (½ hr.); 2 hr. or more (2 hr.). Where time is not indicated, preparation takes between ½ hr. and 2 hr.

Recipes—Serve 12	Page Ref.	Menu Item	Main Ingred.	Ease of Prep.*	Total Prep. Time†	Origin
Garlic French Bread	146	bread	bread, garlic salt	B	½ hr.	
Gingerbread	116	dessert	molasses, sour milk, flour	E		
Gingerbread and Applesauce Cobbler	117	dessert	mix, applesauce	B		
Green Salads	159	salad	wild greens	A		
Gypsy Stew	64	main	ham, soup	B		
Ham	93	main	ham	E	½ hr.	
Ham in a Hole	129	main	ham, vegetable	A	2 hrs.	
Ham Kabobs	90	main	ham, sweet potatoes, pineapple chunks	E		
Ham with Yams and Pineapple	129	main	ham, yams, pineapple	A	2 hrs.	
Hamburger Dinner	144	main	beef, vegetable	E		
Hamburger Supreme	128	main	beef, vegetable	A	2 hrs.	
Hawaiian Islands	75	dessert	bread, pineapple	B	½ hr.	
Heavenly Hot Dogs	91	main	hot dogs, bacon, cheese	E	½ hr.	
Hike Komac	64	main	bacon, soup, beans	B		N.W. U.S.
Hiker's Knapsack	88	main	ham, cheese, pineapple	E	½ hr.	

* Beginner (B); Experienced (E); Advanced (A).
† Includes fire-building time; ½ hr. or less (½ hr.); 2 hr. or more (2 hr.). Where time is not indicated, preparation takes between ½ hr. and 2 hr.

Recipes—Serve 12	Page Ref.	Menu Item	Main Ingred.	Ease of Prep.*	Total Prep. Time†	Origin
Hominy	48	vegetable	green corn	A	2 hrs.	
Honey Butter	47	sauce	butter, honey	B	½ hr.	
Honey Muffins	115	bread	honey, flour	E		
Honey Raisin Brittle	81	candy	rice, sugar	E		
Hopping John	69	main	black-eyed peas, bacon, rice	E	½ hr.	S.E. U.S.
Hot Dogs Supreme	91	main	frankfurters, bacon	E	½ hr.	
Hush Puppies	48	bread	cornmeal, onion	A		S.E. U.S.
Ice Cream (Hay Hole)	41	dessert	evaporated milk, graham cracker crumbs	A	2 hrs.	
Individual Pizzas	106	main	salami, biscuit mix, cheese, tomatoes	B		
Italian Salad	37	salad	lettuce, salami, cheese	B	½ hr.	
Jungle Stew	63	main	beans, macaroni, beef	B		
Kabobs	90	main	beef, bacon, vegetable	E		
Kala Mojakkaa	53	main	fish, vegetable	E		Finland
Karbonade Kaker	59	main	beef	B	½ hr.	Norway
Kartoffel Pfannkuchen	71	main	potatoes, onions, eggs	E		Germany

*Beginner (B); Experienced (E); Advanced (A).
†Includes fire-building time; ½ hr. or less (½ hr.); 2 hr. or more (2 hr.). Where time is not indicated, preparation takes between ½ hr. and 2 hr.

Recipes—Serve 12	Page Ref.	Menu Item	Main Ingred.	Ease of Prep.*	Total Prep. Time†	Origin
Kidney Beans and Spaghetti	68	main	beans, spaghetti, tomatoes	E	2 hrs.	
Komac Stew	59	main	eggs, vegetable	E		
Kraut and Spareribs	140	main	spareribs, vegetable	E		
Laks Laade	106	fish	potatoes, bread, salmon	E		Sweden
Lamb (see Shish Kabobs)		main		E		
Lemonade	43	beverage	lemons	B	½ hr.	
Lettuce Dressing	38	salad	vegetables	B	½ hr.	
Liha Mojakkaa	60, 132	main	beef, vegetables	A	2 hrs.	Finland
Lima Beans and Bacon	130	main	dry limas, bacon	A	2 hrs.	
Liver Kabobs	90	main	liver, bacon	E		
Lyonnaise Potatoes	145	vegetable	potatoes, onions	E		
Macaroni and Cheese	103	main	macaroni, cheese	E		
Mallow Squares	41	dessert	graham crackers, marshmallows, nuts, evaporated milk	B	½ hr.	
Marguerites	118	dessert	saltines, marshmallows	B	½ hr.	
Marshmallow Apple	97	dessert	apples, marshmallows	B	½ hr.	
Meal-in-a-Hole	132	main	beef, vegetables, apples	A	2 hrs.	

*Beginner (B); Experienced (E); Advanced (A).
†Includes fire-building time; ½ hr. or less (½ hr.); 2 hr. or more (2 hr.). Where time is not indicated, preparation takes between ½ hr. and 2 hr.

Recipes—Serve 12	Page Ref.	Menu Item	Main Ingred.	Ease of Prep.*	Total Prep. Time†	Origin
Meal-on-a-Stick	88	main	beef, bread crumbs	E		
Meat Loaf	106	main	beef, evaporated milk	B		
Mexican Enchiladas	58	main	tomatoes, meat, cornmeal, cheese	A		Mexico
Mint and Sorrel Leaf Wafers	34	candy	leaves, egg whites	A	2 hrs.	
Minted Marshmallows	96	dessert	marshmallows, mint wafers	B	½ hr.	
Mock Angel Food Cake	97	dessert	bread, coconut, condensed milk	E	½ hr.	
Molasses Pudding	119	dessert	bread, molasses	B		New England
Molasses Taffy	80	candy	molasses, vinegar	E		
Muffins	114	bread	flour, salad oil	E		
Muffins (made with mix)	114	bread	biscuit mix	B	½ hr.	
Mulligan Stew	132	main	beef, vegetables	A	2 hrs.	
Mulligan Stew	62	main	beef, lamb, vegetables	E	2 hrs.	
Nalasniki	74	main	eggs, flour, cottage cheese	A		Poland
New England Chowder	55	main	clams, fat, pork, vegetables	A	2 hrs.	New England
Norwegian Prune Pudding	75	dessert	prunes, cinnamon, cornstarch	E	2 hrs.	Norway

198

* Beginner (B); Experienced (E); Advanced (A).
† Includes fire-building time; ½ hr. or less (½ hr.); 2 hr. or more (2 hr.). Where time is not indicated, preparation takes between ½ hr. and 2 hr.

Recipes—Serve 12	Page Ref.	Menu Item	Main Ingred.	Ease of Prep.*	Total Prep. Time†	Origin
One-Hundred-Year-Old Johnnycake	118	bread	flour, cornmeal, sour milk	E		Rhode Island
Orange and Date	36	salad	dates, cheese, oranges	B	½ hr.	
Orange Gingerbread	154	dessert	mix, orange	E		
Orange Sweet Potatoes	154	vegetable, dessert	sweet potatoes, oranges, marshmallows	E		
Orangeade	43	beverage	oranges	B	½ hr.	
Oven Drumsticks	107	main	beef, crackers	B		
Oyster Kabobs	90	fish	oysters, bacon	E		
Pan Popped Corn	79	snack	popcorn	B	½ hr.	
Parsley Dressing	39	salad	parsley, onion	B	½ hr.	
Peanut Butter Bread	112	bread	flour, peanut butter	E		
Peppers with Corn	108	main	peppers, corn	E	2 hrs.	
Peppers with Meat	108	main	peppers, beef	E		
Pigs in Blankets (foil)	144	main	flour, sausages	E		
Pigs in Blankets	89	main	flour, sausages	E		
Pink Lemonade	160	beverage	sumac	A		
Pioneer Drumsticks	89	main	beef, eggs, cornflakes	E	½ hr.	

*Beginner (B); Experienced (E); Advanced (A).
†Includes fire-building time; ½ hr. or less (½ hr.); 2 hr. or more (2 hr.). Where time is not indicated, preparation takes between ½ hr. and 2 hr.

Recipes—Serve 12	Page Ref.	Menu Item	Main Ingred.	Ease of Prep.*	Total Prep. Time†	Origin
Planked Fish	92	fish	fish	A		
Planked Steak	92	main	beef	A		
Pocket Stew	63	main	vegetables, bouillon cubes	B		
Poet and Peasant	65	vegetable	onions, apples	B	½ hr.	
Pommes Au Riz	120	dessert	apples, brown sugar, lemon, rice	E		Canada
Popcorn Balls	78	candy	popcorn, molasses	E		
Pork Chops in a Coffee Can	140	main	pork chops	E		
Potato and Frankfurter	29	salad	frankfurters potatoes, tomatoes	B	½ hr.	
Potatoes Baked in Tin Cans	141	vegetable	potatoes	E		
Potato-Onions	145	vegetable	potatoes, onions	E		
Pralines	80	candy	brown sugar, pecans	E		S.E. U.S.
Prune Whip	40	dessert	prunes, lemon, sugar	B	2 hrs.	
Raw Vegetable	31	salad	vegetables	B	½ hr.	
Ribeto	67	main	rice, beef, soup	B		
Ring-Tum-Diddy	66	main	corn, tomatoes, bacon	B		
Sally Lunn Muffins	115	bread	eggs, flour	E		
Salmon Steak	93	fish	salmon	B		

*Beginner (B); Experienced (E); Advanced (A).
†Includes fire-building time; ½ hr. or less (½ hr.); 2 hr. or more (2 hr.). Where time is not indicated, preparation takes between ½ hr. and 2 hr.

Recipes—Serve 12	Page Ref.	Menu Item	Main Ingred.	Ease of Prep.*	Total Prep. Time†	Origin
Salmon Wiggle	56	main	salmon, peas	B		
Sandwich Fillings	29	sandwich		B	½ hr.	
Sausage and Spaghetti	68	main	sausages, spaghetti	B		
Sauté Chipped Beef with Bananas	57	main	beef, bananas	E	½ hr.	
Savoy Beans	65	main	sausages, beans, vegetables	E		
Scalloped Chipped Beef and Potatoes	105	main	flour, potatoes, beef	E		
Scalloped Ham with Potatoes and Onions	128	main	ham, vegetables	A	2 hrs.	
Scrambled Eggs and Corn	51	main	corn, eggs	B	½ hr.	
Shish Kabobs	90	main	lamb, vegetables	E		Near East
Short-Cut Fudge	76	candy	unsweetened chocolate, condensed milk	B	½ hr.	
Shredded Cabbage	56	vegetable	cabbage	B	½ hr.	
Shrimp Barbecue	143	fish	shrimp, garlic	E		
Snow Bread	111	bread	flour, snow	A		
Snow Corn Bread	111	bread	cornmeal, snow	A		
Snow on the Mountain	79	dessert	chocolate bars, coconut	B	½ hr.	
Snowballs	79	dessert	sour milk, nutmeg, flour	A	½ hr.	

* Beginner (B); Experienced (E); Advanced (A).
† Includes fire-building time; ½ hr. or less (½ hr.); 2 hr. or more (2 hr.). Where time is not indicated, preparation takes between ½ hr. and 2 hr.

Recipes—Serve 12	Page Ref.	Menu Item	Main Ingred.	Ease of Prep.*	Total Prep. Time†	Origin
Some-Mores	98	dessert	marshmallows, graham crackers, chocolate bars	E	½ hr.	
Soups	160	soup	wild foods	A		
Sour Cream Salad Dressing	39	salad	sour cream, lemon	B	½ hr.	
Sour Dough Bread	110	bread	flour, vinegar	A	2 hrs.	
South Sea Delight	122	dessert	bananas, oranges, coconut	E		
Southern Goulash	61	main	beef broth, beef, spaghetti	E		S.E. U.S.
Spanish Rice	71	main	rice, bacon tomatoes	E		
Spice Cake	116	dessert	flour, spices	E		
Spiced Milk	81	beverage	cinnamon, milk	B	½ hr.	
Spider Corn Bread	50	bread	eggs, cornmeal	E		N.W. U.S.
Spinach and Orange	32	salad	spinach, oranges	B	½ hr.	
Spoon Bread	109	bread	cornmeal, eggs	E		S.E. U.S.
Squaw Corn	69	main	bacon, corn	B	½ hr.	
Steamed Canned Corn and Bacon	145	main	corn, bacon	E	½ hr.	
Stuffed Trout	143	fish	fish, onions	E		

* Beginner (B); Experienced (E); Advanced (A).
† Includes fire-building time; ½ hr. or less (½ hr.); 2 hr. or more (2 hr.). Where time is not indicated, preparation takes between ½ hr. and 2 hr.

Recipes—Serve 12	Page Ref.	Menu Item	Main Ingred.	Ease of Prep.*	Total Prep. Time†	Origin
Submarine (Hero) Sandwiches	145	main	bread (long), filling		½ hr.	
Sugaring Off	80	candy	maple sirup	E		N.E. U.S.
Sweet Potato and Apples	104	vegetable	sweet potatoes, apples	E		
Sweet Potato and Orange Casserole	104	vegetable	sweet potatoes, oranges	E		
Sweet Potato Casseroles (embers)	140	main	sweet potatoes, apples or oranges	E		
Tea (Hot)	161	beverage	wild foods	A	½ hr.	
Teriyaki	90	main	pineapple chunks, beef	E		Japan
Thousand Island Dressing	39	salad	eggs, mayonnaise	B	½ hr.	
Toasted Taffy Apples	97	dessert	apple, brown sugar	B	½ hr.	
Toasts	96	bread, breakfast, dessert	bread, toppings	B	½ hr.	
Tomato Rarebit	67	main	tomatoes, cheese, eggs	E		
Tortillas	49	bread	cornmeal, flour	A		Mexico
Tossed Salad	33	salad	celery, greens	B	½ hr.	
Veal Chops or Cutlets	140	main	veal	E		

*Beginner (B); Experienced (E); Advanced (A).
†Includes fire-building time; ½ hr. or less (½ hr.); 2 hr. or more (2 hr.). Where time is not indicated, preparation takes between ½ hr. and 2 hr.

Recipes—Serve 12	Page Ref.	Menu Item	Main Ingred.	Ease of Prep.*	Total Prep. Time†	Origin
Venetian Eggs	52	main	tomatoes, eggs, salt pork, cheese	E		
Vienna Eggs	155	breakfast, main	sausages, eggs	E	½ hr.	
Volcano Potatoes	104	main	potatoes, cheese	E		
Waldorf Salad	32	salad	apples, celery, nuts	B	½ hr.	
Walking Salad	33	salad	apples, cheese	B	½ hr.	
Water Boiled in a Bag	156	beverage	water	A	½ hr.	
Wild Rice	160	vegetable	wild rice	A		
Wild Fruit Jelly and Jams	160	garnish	wild foods	A		
Yoki Special	71	main	bacon, tomatoes, spaghetti, cheese	B		

* Beginner (B); Experienced (E); Advanced (A).
† Includes fire-building time; ½ hr. or less (½ hr.); 2 hr. or more (2 hr.). Where time is not indicated, preparation takes between ½ hr. and 2 hr.

GENERAL INDEX

P.D. 6-60
1-71

NOTES

NOTES

NOTES

NOTES

210

NOTES

NOTES

NOTES

NOTES

NOTES

215

NOTES